Accounting Made Easy with Your Computer

Understanding the Buzzwords and Basics of Accounting Using Today's Most Popular Software

Jean E. Gutmann

Sourcebooks, Inc.

Naperville, IL

Sample reports and screen captures from Peachtree® and One-Write Plus® used with permission of Peachtree Software.

Sample reports and screen captures from QuickBooks® software used with permission of Intuit®.

Sample specification list for M.Y.O.B.® used with permission from BestWare®.

This publication is designed to provide accurate and authoritative information in regard to the subject matter covered. It is sold with the understanding that the publisher is not engaged in rendering legal, accounting, or other professional service. If legal advice or other expert assistance is required, the services of a competent professional person should be sought.

From a Declaration of Principles Jointly Adopted by a Committee of the American Bar Association and a Committee of Publishers and Associations

Published by Sourcebooks
P.O. Box 372
Naperville, Illinois 60566
(630) 961-3900
FAX: 630-961-2168

 Sourcebooks, Inc.

Naperville, IL

Library of Congress Cataloging-in-Publication Data

Gutmann, Jean E.
    Accounting made easy with your computer: understanding the buzzwords and basics of accounting using today's most popular software / Jean E. Gutmann.
        p.   cm.
        Includes index.
        ISBN   1-57071-126-7
        1. Accounting—Data processing.   2. Accounting—Computer programs.
    I. Title.
    HF5679.G88   1998
    657'.0285'536—dc21   97-29466
                                                        CIP

Printed and Bound in the United States of America
10 9 8 7 6 5 4 3 2

Contents

List of Figures

Acknowledgments

In Gratitude

This book comes to you as a coherent and helpful document because so many terrific people assisted me with it. First and foremost, I would like to extend a huge shout of THANKS to Barbara MacNeil Jones, a small business accounting consultant at the Eastern Maine Development Center in Bangor, Maine, who read all of the chapters and provided detailed suggestions and improvements. Other folks who read the draft manuscript and made significant contributions are Connie Morin of Stratton, Maine, Kelly Wilkinson of W. Forks, Maine, and John Sanders and Karen Walton of Portland, Maine. I am also indebted to my colleagues Mark Lapping, Jim Westfall, Chuck Davis, and John Burt at the University of Southern Maine, who lent considerable support and encouragement.

Todd Stocke, my editor at Sourcebooks, was caring and persistent in his support of the project—and I want to thank him from the bottom of my heart. Many other folks at Sourcebooks, especially Ro Sila and Beth Peluso, invested Herculean effort to make this the best book we could write for you. Thanks!

Trademarks

All brand names and product names used in this book are trademarks, registered trademarks, copyrights, or trade names of their respective current owners. Sourcebooks, Inc., is not associated with any of these products or vendors. We wish to extend our thanks to Peachtree Software and Intuit, Inc., for their cooperation in granting permission to illustrate their products in this book.

Windows® is a registered trademark of Microsoft Corporation.

One-Write Plus® is a registered trademark of Peachtree Software, Inc.

Peachtree® is a registered trademark of Peachtree Software, Inc.

QuickBooks® and Quicken® are registered trademarks of Intuit, Inc.

Microsoft Money is owned by Microsoft Corporation.

Business Works® is a registered trademark of State of the Art Software, Inc.

Quattro® Pro is a registered trademark of Corel Corporation.

WordPerfect® is a registered trademark of Corel Corporation.

M.Y.O.B.® is a registered trademark of BW-VA, Inc.

Preface

About This Book

Any person interested in accounting software—a small business owner or office manager, a student of accounting, a small business consultant, or a practicing accountant trying to help small businesses—will find this book most useful as a reference tool. Scan the Table of Contents, read the items most relevant to your current needs, then keep *Accounting Made Easy with Your Computer* on the shelf above your computer to look up specific procedures as you need the information. Those contemplating or assisting with the purchase of accounting software might want to read the book in order, from Chapter 1 through Chapter 11, to get the full picture of how the important functions of accounting are performed by the computer.

Suggestions for Using This Book

Chapters 1 and 2 introduce the uses of small business accounting software and describes the process for acquiring software. All accounting uses a "General Ledger" as its basis, and Chapter 3 will explain this sometimes confusing accounting tool. After reading these three chapters, I would direct you to the Table of Contents to decide which part of an accounting system is most important to you. If collecting revenue from your credit customers is most important to you, then go to Chapter 7 where the concepts of sales invoicing and collecting accounts receivable are presented. If payroll is your biggest worry, go to Chapter 9. In other words, the chapters don't have to be read in order! After reading the first three chapters, you can go directly to any topic.

Chapter One

Small Business Accounting and Computers

Understanding Accounting and Computers

Accounting is the function that helps small business people focus on business management goals such as increasing sales, managing cash flow, collecting receivables, controlling payables, and monitoring key business functions. This book will enhance your understanding of the "accounting magic" that is performed by today's powerful—but low-cost—software. This is not a computer book, so it assumes that you know a little about computers and probably already have one in place at your office. For clarity, however, this chapter starts with some discussion of the important buzzwords of personal computer (PC) hardware. Otherwise, hardware will rarely be mentioned later in the book. It is software (computer programs) that allows your computer to handle your accounting tasks, so this book focuses primarily on that software.

What Is Accounting Software?

First of all, let's be sure that you know the meaning of the word software: software is the collection of detailed computer instructions (called a program) that leads the electronic circuits through the steps of processing raw data into useful information. An example would be the payroll software that takes in employee data and puts out your weekly paycheck. Software is stored on hard disks or CD-ROM and brought into internal computer memory (called RAM) when you need it to perform tasks. (These acronyms are defined later in this chapter.)

Accounting software is designed to maintain accounting records in businesses large and small. First are the universal tasks of maintaining ledgers and recording transactions, ranging from sales and purchases to investments by owners and recording of depreciation. It also might include less common accounting procedures like tracking job order costs or producing an annual income tax return. The most common functions handled by accounting software are:

- sales invoicing
- accounts receivable tracking
- purchasing control
- check writing
- accounts payable management
- payroll recording
- inventory tracking

This book focuses on these most common activities. We'll talk more about the definition of software categories later in this chapter, and much more about accounting software functions in Chapter 2.

Introduction to Small Business Computers

The Buzzwords

Here is a typical sales pitch at a computer store: "You really need a Pentium chip with 16 megabytes of RAM—expandable to 64, running at 200 megahertz, for Windows 95 and Netscape, and if you're going to expect DDE for your Peachtree reports and database software, you better plan on CD-ROM and a memory cache of 8 megabytes." Whew! Just getting to the right accounting package may expose you to the headache of hardware choices. You don't need to know what all that jargon means, but assuming you are a computer novice, let's start out with the minimum vocabulary you need to make your first software purchase.

Hardware

Hardware is the collective term used to encompass all the physical parts (especially electronic) that make up your computer system. The most familiar hardware parts are the keyboard, mouse, screen, and printer. The "system unit," however, which contains the circuit boards that make up memory and control wiring, is the most important part.

The only technical computer terms you need to know to run your accounting software are:

- the type of operating system your computer uses
- the memory (internal storage) the software requires
- the hard disk or CD-ROM space the software needs

Operating Systems

An operating system is built into all modern microcomputers (also called PCs or personal computers). Yours probably has either MS-DOS, Windows, or an Macintosh operating system. The operating system is programmed into the circuits of the computer and/or stored in a secure (that is, read-only and non-erasable) part of the hard disk. The operating system is a computer program that wakes up your computer when you turn the computer on and then presents you with an organized menu (or screen full of small pictures called "icons") from which you select the software you want to run. The operating system also manages all the files you store in memory and on disk and sends control messages to other hardware like the printer. The most-used operating system is Windows.

MS-DOS stands for Microsoft-Disk Operating System. It was invented by Microsoft and is found on all IBM PCs and PC clones. MS-DOS has now been largely hidden by the Windows operating system. The Windows operating system presents a graphic (pictorial) environment where you use your mouse to click on choices and use your keyboard to type information in small boxes called windows. The Windows environment allows you to have many windows open at one time to operate several computer programs simultaneously, exchanging information between programs when needed. Windows is quickly becoming the preferred operating system for small businesses.

Apple Corporation went its own way (not mirroring MS-DOS) and created the Macintosh operating system, which relied on graphic screen design from the start (before Microsoft introduced Windows). Apple has improved its operating systems through the Macintosh System 7, System 7.5, and now System 8. The Macintosh operating system makes effective use of icons instead of text-based menus and allows you to work with several programs simultaneously.

The software packages described in this book come in either a Windows or Macintosh version, which look pretty much the same. Three Windows packages are showcased in this book.

Windows

To get a better feel for the layout of a "window" and the graphic operating system, refer to Figure 1-1. This is an example of a screen from the QuickBooks for Windows software. Here you can see a window within a window; the area surrounded by a heavy black box is the active window. Thus the "format header/footer" window is where you are currently working. In this illustration, the user is expected to make various choices in order to customize a report. You can type text in some boxes or click on options to produce a customized result. Notice that you can type in your own report title and/or specify whether you want page numbers on the report. When you point and click on the small white boxes with your mouse, you check (use) or uncheck (ignore) them.

A toolbar contains icons that represent available functions. In Figure 1-1, the "invoice" icon allows you to create sales invoices, the "check" icon allows you to create checks, the "calc" icon provides you with an on-screen calculator, etc. Also notice the lines below the "format header/footer" window ("interest expense," etc.)—this is another window in the background that is displaying the report you are currently working on. We'll see many more examples of the Windows and Macintosh graphic displays throughout this book.

Figure 1-1: *Sample Windows screen*

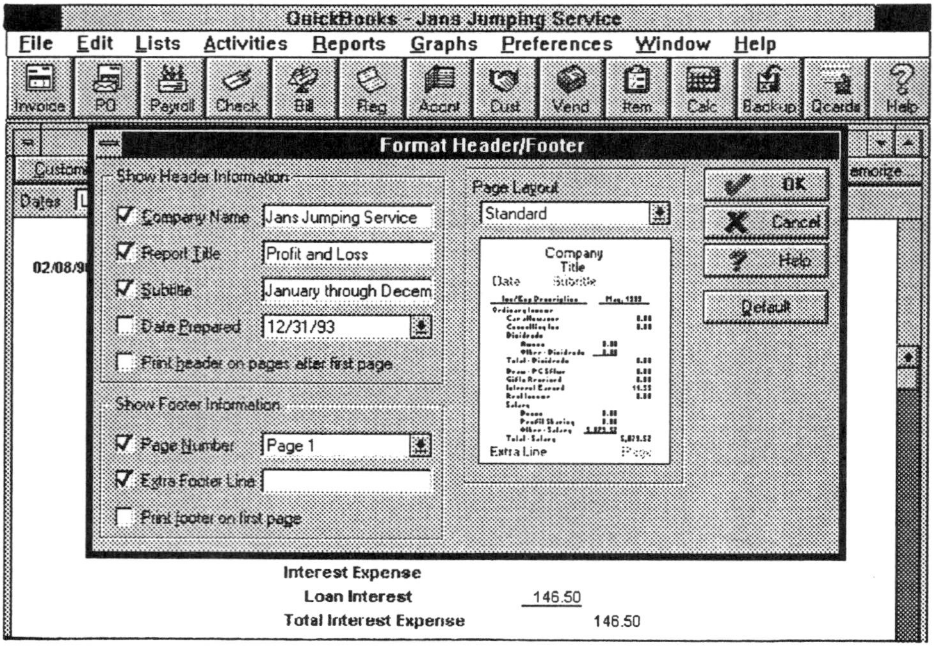

Memory

Memory refers to the places inside your computer where programs and data are stored while you are working within a specific software package. These "places" are within the integrated circuits called microchips.

RAM is the Random Access Memory inside a computer. This is called "Random Access Memory" because data can be quickly and easily retrieved from it, without having to search from A to Z, and because you can write in it and easily erase it. In fact, RAM is erased every time you turn the power off because it relies on the presence of electricity. (The contents of RAM may be permanently stored on hard disk or CD-ROM. See below.) The Windows operating system and most small business accounting packages require at least 8MB of RAM. MB stands for a million bytes and one byte stores one character of information; so 8MB is storage space for 8 million characters of information. Contemporary computers are now sold with at least 8MB of RAM. Even if you only have 4MB of RAM, you can still run most Windows accounting packages, but they will seem to run extremely slow.

Hard Disk and CD-ROM

The other kind of storage that a computer needs is the permanent kind— a secure place that will not be erased until you want it to be. Hard disk and CD-ROM (compact disk, read-only memory) provide long-term storage; their contents are not lost when the electricity is turned off. With a hard disk and some writable CDs, you can direct the computer to write on them at your convenience. Both hard disks and CD-ROM are used to "hold" accounting software programs until you give the command to load them into RAM for your use.

The setup for all of the newest software copies the program instructions from diskettes or CD onto your hard disk. Hard disks now come in sizes ranging from 540MB to 850MB and even 1 to 3GB (gigabytes)—that's billions of bytes! The software showcased in this book occupies from 10 to 25MB of hard disk space plus another 5 to 10 MB for your data, so you should have no problem with disk size, even if your computer has an older 120MB or 240MB hard disk, as long as you are not simultaneously running too many other programs such as word processing, spreadsheet, time management, or computer games.

If you choose an accounting package that runs on CD-ROM only, a small portion of the loading instructions will have to reside on your hard disk (usually 1 to 2MB), but the CD will have to be inserted in the CD-ROM drive whenever you are using the package. At startup, a large portion of the program is copied into RAM, and some special procedures are later called up from the CD as needed. The CD-ROM alternative saves you hard disk space and is very fast in storage and retrieval of data and program instructions.

Small Business Computer Applications

Small businesses have put computers to many uses. "Computer applications" is the generic term we use to describe the tasks that computers can handle for us. If you didn't buy your computer to do accounting tasks, then you probably started with word processing. Accounting, word processing, spreadsheets, database management, contact management, time management, timekeeping, income tax planning, income tax returns, manufacturing management, and computer aided design (CAD) are all examples of computer applications. Today the Internet and the World Wide Web are two new computer applications that small businesses are plugging into with their PCs. And whole books have already been written to help you use the "Web" for a business advantage.

Of course, this book is about accounting applications for computers. If you haven't yet purchased an accounting package, you will find a lot of helpful information in Chapter 2 to aid you in your search for the right software; and some hints on how to get started with it.

Small Business Accounting

The accounting functions that are performed most religiously by small businesses are checkbook maintenance and the production of invoices to bill customers. In order to produce a Profit and Loss Statement (sometimes called the Income Statement), you need to know your revenue and expenses. In order to track these revenue and expenses, you need to maintain a set of accounts in an arrangement called a general ledger. Whether you do this manually (with pencil and paper) or use a computer, you will find that many useful management reports can be gleaned from the information in your general ledger to answer such questions as:

- Do you need better control of cash flow or inventory?
- Do you write your own payroll checks?
- Do you need to prepare sales invoices?

Getting a clear financial picture of your business is why you want an accounting software package. The small business accounting tasks that draw that picture are the subject of this book.

Types of Accounting Packages

Low-End Packages (under $300)

This book uses three of the low-end accounting packages to familiarize you with computerized accounting procedures. The most widely used of these are CheckMark Multi-Ledger, DacEasy, M.Y.O.B. (for Mind Your Own Business), One-Write Plus, Peachtree, and QuickBooks. All of these are "Windows" programs for IBM-PCs or compatibles, or are Macintosh programs, or they come in a version for each type of system. All of these packages sell for less than $300, and Appendix A lists addresses and phone numbers for the companies that sell them. The programs in this category all provide a company with a general ledger as the basic unit of storage, with sub-ledgers for customers, vendors, employees, jobs, and inventory items. You will hear much more about these types of packages as you read further in this book.

Full-Featured Packages ($395 per module to more than $5,000 for a system)

Accounting packages that are designed for medium to large size businesses are normally sold by the module. That is, you would purchase the general ledger module or system module separate from the accounts receivable module, and each module is priced separately. For example, a program called Business Works by State of the Art Software sold for $395 per module in 1997, with a start-up deal offered at $995 that included a systems module, general ledger, accounts receivable, and accounts payable. As you add on their order entry or fixed asset module you pay $395 for each. Other vendors in this category are Great Plains Software, Solomon, Computer Associates, and Platinum Accounting Systems. These types of packages are known as "high-end" or full featured packages. Their level of sophistication and complexity goes far beyond that of the low-end packages. However, they all follow the same basic accounting principles that are described in this book. Refer to Appendix A for names and addresses of some of these software vendors.

Custom Programming ($20,000 or more)

Sometimes the "off the shelf" software (all of those described above) just won't fill all your accounting needs. Very large corporations have built their accounting systems from scratch by hiring systems analysts and computer programmers who design custom applications. Even when a small business buys Peachtree or QuickBooks, they sometimes hire a computer programmer to add to its features by writing custom computer routines. This option is very expensive and time consuming. This book assumes that you are not currently a candidate for this complex and costly aspect of computerized accounting.

Electronic Checkbooks Are Not Accounting Software

There are some very popular record keeping programs in use by small businesses that are not accounting programs because they do not maintain full account ledgers and have no capacity for managing accounts receivable (customer accounts) or accounts payable (vendor accounts). These computer programs are classified as electronic checkbooks. The main purpose of Quicken and Microsoft Money, the most popular electronic checkbook programs, is to allow you to write checks and keep track of the categories of expenditures for those checks, and to manage other accounts like credit cards and investment portfolios. They do not work as debit/credit systems and do not follow generally accepted accounting principles.

Software Featured in This Book

I have been using, teaching about, and consulting on accounting software for twenty years. During that time, I have worked with hummers and bummers. In the past year, I invested a huge number of hours in testing and choosing three software packages that would be suitable for this book and that I could present to you as very desirable choices that fit a wide variety of small business types. It is my intention to demystify accounting procedures for you. This book offers examples for various accounting functions from One-Write Plus for Windows, Peachtree for Windows, and QuickBooks for Windows. Explanations of those functions are written in plain, simple English. Although this book is not a tutorial on how to use any of these packages (you can get that from the user's manual for any of them), I will explain the accounting concepts behind the procedures these packages perform, and I will help you figure out which functions you need and which you don't (something the user's manual will not tell you).

Peachtree for Windows

Peachtree for Windows includes modules for general ledger, purchase orders, accounts payable, sales invoices, accounts receivable, inventory, payroll, and job cost accounting. In 1997, it sold for a suggested retail price of $129 for Windows or $99 for Macintosh when purchased directly from Peachtree. It has received many "editor's pick" awards and "best buy" recommendations from popular computer magazines. I consider this program to be the most robust and comprehensive of the three packages included here; it is ready to be run on a network (two or more computers linked electronically, which share software and data) to be used by multiple users. It is easy to use, has a good screen design, and can be customized in many ways. Its SmartFill (for automated data entry) and drill down (to look behind the lines on reports for more complete information and data) capabilities are outstanding. The Peachtree user's manuals are often judged the best in the industry and include a helpful booklet, titled "Accounting Primer," written by a Harvard accounting professor. Peachtree is the oldest name in small business accounting software; Peachtree for DOS has been in use around the country since the mid 1970s.

QuickBooks for Windows

QuickBooks for Windows is a more recent entry in the Windows accounting software market, although its predecessor, QuickBooks for DOS, has been around since about 1985. This package (from Intuit, Inc.) sells for a suggested retail of $99.95 for the Windows version or $119.95 for the Macintosh version. There is a more sophisticated version called QuickBooks Pro (for Macintosh or Windows), with additional business software and true job order cost accounting for about $199. QuickBooks became very popular because it is easy to upgrade from the popular Quicken checkbook program, which claims millions of users. The latest version of QuickBooks includes general ledger, accounts receivable, accounts payable, payroll, inventory, and project cost modules. It handles purchase orders, many types of invoices, and many types of lists (including sales tax rates, payroll deduction items, payment terms, etc.). In my opinion, this program is the easiest to use of the three included here, although it is not very sophisticated in the areas of payroll or inventory management. It has an uncluttered screen design and is very user friendly, with helpful error messages, reminders to make backup copies, and excellent context sensitive help. QuickBooks is not network ready, but it is available in both a Windows and Macintosh version.

One-Write Plus for Windows

One-Write Plus for Windows was released in December of 1995, although One-Write Plus for DOS has been around since the late 1980s and has a very large user base. This (Peachtree Software) program sells for a suggested retail of $89.95 and includes general ledger, accounts receivable, accounts payable, inventory, job cost tracking, and payroll functions. The design of this package is based on a manual check writing system where the check form, carbon paper, and additional forms are layered on top of one another so that you write the transaction once and the data is recorded in several places. The One-Write Plus package is easy to use and provides very simple automated setup and tutorials. I find the screen layout to be very crowded, with some forms (invoices, purchase orders, and reports) falling off the edges of the screen. This package is not ready to be run on a network and is not available in a Macintosh version.

A Word about Prices

The prices given in the preceding three paragraphs were quoted to me by the vendors in mid 1997. The suggested retail prices of software packages are usually higher than their "street prices." Usually the best place to buy accounting software is through mail order houses or discount office supply stores where you will find the prices to be $10–$50 less than the suggested retail.

Accounting Software Features

When I speak of "features," I refer to the selling points that make a piece of software clear and easy to work with. The help system of a package, its screen layout, its menu system, the methods you use to enter data, special quick key combinations, and the user prompts you see on screen are all items that are considered to be software features. For example, QuickBooks assists you during data entry with its QuickFill feature. QuickFill uses the master files (e.g., customer file) to fill in all appropriate data for that customer as soon as you type the first few letters of the customer name. This works with vendors, employees, accounts, inventory items, and many other items that it can look up in its own vast memory. It is the richness, or lack, of these types of features that can make a program worth thousands of dollars to you or make it worthless. We will explore some of these features further in Chapter 2.

Accounting Software Modules

I use the terms "modules" and "systems" interchangeably throughout this book. The word "modules" refers to the distinct parts within an accounting software package. Accounts Receivable tasks would be contained in one module; while Payroll tasks would be contained in another module. Most low-end accounting packages contain the four basic modules:

- general ledger
- accounts payable (including check writing)
- accounts receivable
- payroll

Other modules that are sometimes available are inventory, job order costing, bank reconciliation, and report customization. If a package contains the function of creating and managing purchase orders, this is usually included in the accounts payable module. If a package contains functions for producing sales quotations and sales invoices, this is contained in the accounts receivable module. The check writing function is contained in accounts payable. In other words, there are a lot of subtasks that are contained within each module. The appropriate chapters will provide you with detailed descriptions of and user perspectives on all the above modules.

Some Expert Advice

First and foremost—don't wait any longer to buy a computer and accounting software. Prices have tumbled for both hardware and software. Today's $100 accounting package would have cost $2,000 for equal features and power only ten years ago.

The price of an accounting package is almost insignificant compared to the benefits you will reap from improved efficiency and better control of your finances. The difference between an $89 package and a $199 more advanced package is absolutely zero if you need the features of the $199 program. Pay a hundred dollars more for the ability to export reports to other software or the convenience of importing Macintosh files into your Windows PC—and enjoy the increased efficiency.

The best source of information about what works and what doesn't may be a friend or colleague. Ask around to find someone who has similar accounting needs and who is in a position similar to yours—just getting ready to buy, or just installing a specific program, or suffering through the installation and setup of a specific package, or rolling along rather smoothly with one package but maybe looking for a better one. I will try to address all of these audiences in this book by presenting what you need to know at all of these stages.

If, after reading the parts of this book relevant to your needs, you would like a more in-depth understanding of these accounting functions, consider taking a short accounting or bookkeeping course. Your local community college or high school adult education department may offer regular and computer-based accounting classes. You might meet others who are in the same situation as you are and who will share knowledge (triumphs and tragedies) with you.

Finally, be sure to seek the advice of an accountant on any accounting issues that require adherence to law.

Chapter Two

Choosing and Using Accounting Software

Introduction to Small Business Accounting Software

With hundreds of accounting software packages out there for you to choose from, making the right choice is not easy. I cannot begin or end this chapter with a recommendation on a specific package because so much depends on the needs of your business and the features of the software package. Your accountant should make a recommendation on your software choice only if she or he is fully knowledgeable about your business. All accounting packages are not created equal!

Here are the top ten low-cost accounting packages: AccPac Simply Accounting, Accountant for Windows, Check Mark MultiLedger, DacEasy, M.Y.O.B. (for Mind Your Own Business), One-Write Plus, Pacioli 2000, Peachtree Accounting, Profit (by Great Plains Software), and QuickBooks. Most of these are Windows programs for IBM-PC compatibles, some are for the Macintosh, and some have a version for each operating system. (The terms Windows, IBM-PC, Macintosh, and operating system were explained in Chapter 1.) All of these packages sell for between $80 and $300.

This chapter introduces you to the features of these low-end accounting packages and provides some advice on choosing your package. Once you have chosen your software, of course, you will need to develop a strategy for getting the most from it. Let's explore these topics together.

Analyzing Needs

Common Needs of Small Business

- Do you need better control of your inventory?
- Could you collect more cash from customers and clients with timely and repeat billings for the appropriate target accounts?
- Would you be more comfortable with automatic calculation and accumulation of payroll taxes?
- Do you know how your expenses this month compare to last month or the same month a year ago? How about income comparisons?
- Could you benefit from a clearer picture of your revenue and expenses on a monthly or weekly basis?
- And the quintessential problem of all small businesses: do you know where your cash goes and why you never have enough of it?

All of these questions are ones that a good accounting software package can help you to answer, but the big question is, "What areas are the most important to you?"

Figure 2–1 provides a list and explanation of the most common components of the low-end accounting packages named earlier in this chapter. The term "components" is used to mean tasks that are performed by a module. The most widely used modules are general ledger, accounts payable, accounts receivable, inventory, and payroll. Which components are most important to you?

Figure 2-1: *Components commonly found in accounting software packages for under $300*

General Ledger
Tracks activity in a set of ledger accounts
Transactions in a General Journal
Import/Export Data for all components
Report Customization for all components
Reports: Income Statement, Balance Sheet, and Cash Flow Statement

Accounts Payable
Tracks vendor and purchasing activity
Purchase orders, returns, and allowances
Check writing and expense distribution
Cash Requirements Report
Reports: Vendor Balances, Purchases, and Cash Disbursements Activity

Accounts Receivable
Tracks customer and selling activity
Quotations, invoices, returns, and allowances
Customer invoice and statements
Bank deposit records
Reports: Customer Balances, Aged Receivables, Sales, and Cash Receipts Activity

Payroll
Prepares pay checks
Maintains employee payroll history
Tracks tax deductions and liability to taxing agencies
Produces forms for tax filing requirements
Reports: Payroll Register, Employee Earnings Record, and Payroll Tax Reports

Figure 2-1 cont.

Inventory

Tracks inventory purchase and sales

Inventory on hand, reorder level, and
    reorder quantity

Calculates average unit cost

Applies cost of sales

Inventory sales activity analysis

Reports: Inventory Status, Sales Reports,
    Reorder Lists, Price List, and Physical
    Inventory List

Job/Project Tracking

Track costs and revenue to jobs or projects

Accepts data from General Ledger, Accounts
    Payable, Payroll, and Accounts Receivable

Job/Project Quotations or Estimates

Master file with job dates, customer, supervi-
    sor, sub-contractor liabilities, and reim-
    bursable expenses

Reports: Job Ledger Listing, Job Profitability,
    and Job Transaction Listings

Additional Capabilities

Bank Reconciliation

Credit Card Reconciliation

Depreciation Calculator

Complete Report Customization

Sample Company and Sample Chart of
    Accounts

Guided Tutorial for Startup

Multi-user versions (for network use)

Determining Your Specific Business Needs

The most important step in the decision to buy or upgrade your accounting software is identifying your specific needs. If you are dissatisfied with your current accounting package, it is probably because you didn't match your needs to the features of the software you purchased. So let's talk about needs first, and then we will go on to survey the features of the widely used software.

Use Figure 2–2 to determine what areas within your business are the most critical for short-term automation and repeated benefit from computerization. Photocopy an enlargement of Figure 2–2, go to a quiet place, and take some uninterrupted time to read and mark every single line. Under "Need Level," use an R to signify "absolutely required," a D to mean "desirable, but we can function without it," and an N to mark "items that are not needed." For example, think of your vendor records. Do you need two address fields (one for the "pay to" address and one for the "order from" address)? Do you need space for an e-mail address? A Web site address for ordering? If you handle inventory, do you need software that can handle the LIFO or FIFO methods (most low-cost packages use the average cost method)?

Once you have marked the needs of your business, you can evaluate what you want your accounting software to do for you.

Figure 2-2: *Accounting functions—needs checklist*

For	**Prepared on**
Your Company Name	Date

Mark your level of need on the blank line. For example: R = absolutely required,
D = desirable but not absolutely needed, N = not needed.

Need Level

Customers:

Master File Needs—

____ ID number as well as name
____ Multiple address fields (i.e. sell to, ship to, etc.)
____ Multiple phone numbers (i.e. fax, modem, etc.)
____ E-mail address
____ Associated with jobs/projects
____ Credit limit
____ Produce invoices
____ Produce statements
____ View customer activity (current)
____ View customer history (up to a year back)
____ Aged accounts receivable in detail
____ Aged accounts receivable in summary

Invoicing:

____ Enter quotations or estimates
____ Automatic incremental invoice numbers
____ Recall old invoices for corrections
____ Use multiple selling terms
____ Calculate sales discounts
____ Integrate with inventory file
____ Automated price entry
____ Charge reimbursable expenses to customers
____ Returns and allowances recorded as invoices
____ Automatic sales tax calculation
____ Multiple sales tax jurisdictions
____ Taxable and non-taxable on same invoice
____ Default account numbers used
____ Apply revenue to jobs/projects
____ Handle back orders

Cash Receipts:

____ Apply cash receipts against invoices *or*
____ Balance forward method for each account
____ Apply cash receipts for cash revenue
____ Prepare bank deposit records
____ Use default account numbers for cash inflow
____ View cash account frequently
____ Predict cash receipts for cash forecast

Other Accounts Receivable Needs:

____ Automatic finances charges
____ Choose customers for finance charges
____ Identify sales by salesperson
____ Override discounts
____ Handle commissions

Reports—

____ Sales Journal
____ Cash Receipts Journal
____ Detailed Accounts Receivable Ledger
____ Sales Activity Analysis

____ **Estimate your number of customers**

Need Level

Vendors:

Master File Needs—

____ ID number as well as name
____ Source address and payment address
____ Multiple phone numbers (i.e. fax. modem, etc.)
____ Default GL account numbers
____ E-mail address
____ Vendor's account number
____ 1099 coding
____ Vendor terms for payment
____ Produce debit memos
____ View current vendor activity
____ View vendor history
____ Aged accounts payable in detail
____ Aged accounts payable in summary

Purchase Activity:

____ Prepare purchase orders
____ Turn purchase orders into invoices
____ Enter invoices from vendors
____ Handles returns/adjustments
____ Integrate with inventory file
____ Tie in to jobs/projects
____ Charge reimbursable expenses to customers

Check Writing:

____ Apply checks to outstanding invoices
____ Apply checks directly to expense
____ Compute discounts
____ Flag payments on due dates
____ Default account numbers for vendors
____ Recurring check transactions
____ Enter manual checks without printing
____ Print checks one at a time *or*
____ Print checks in a batch
____ Automatic and incremental check numbering
____ Mandatory void check accounting

Other Accounts Payable Needs:

____ 1099 Vendors, with year-end forms
____ Bank reconciliation
____ Credit card reconciliation

Reports—

____ Purchases Journal
____ Cash Disbursements Journal
____ Open Purchase Orders
____ Detailed Accounts Payable Ledger
____ Purchase Activity Report
____ Cash Requirements Report

____ **Estimate your number of vendors**

Figure 2-2 cont.

Need Level	Inventory:
	Inventory Item File—
_____	Item ID number as well as name
_____	Item description
_____	Sales price field
_____	Automatic sale price based on cost +
_____	Automatic sales tax code
_____	Automatic average cost calculation, *or*
_____	Other unit cost calculation (LIFO, FIFO)
_____	Reorder level
_____	Reorder quantity
_____	Automatic purchase orders for inventory reorder
_____	View item activity and/or history
	Reports—
_____	Price List
_____	Inventory Status Report
_____	Inventory Reorder List

Inventory Data Entry:
(Inventory data entry happens in sales, purchases, payroll, and general ledger)

Need Level	
_____	Pop-up inventory item file during data entry
_____	New items entered on-the-fly
_____	Sales transactions apply cost of sales

Other Inventory Needs:

Need Level	
_____	Maintain inventory valuation
_____	Inventory sales activity analysis
_____	Assembly data for manufacturing company
	Other Reports—
_____	Physical Inventory List
_____	Inventory Profitability Report
_____	Inventory graphs

_____	**Estimate your number of inventory items**

General Ledger:

Need Level	
_____	More than five digit account numbers
_____	One level of sub-accounts
_____	Two levels of sub-accounts
_____	Three levels of sub-accounts
_____	General Journal item descriptions
_____	Income Statement
_____	Balance Sheet
_____	Statement of Cash Flows
_____	Trial Balance
_____	Detailed General Ledger printout
_____	Financial Statement graphs
_____	Printed General Journal
_____	Maintain budgets
_____	Report budget comparative analysis

Job/Project Tracking:

Need Level	
	Job/Project Master File—
_____	Job/Project ID number as well as name
_____	Start date, end date, critical dates
_____	Job salesperson or supervisor name
_____	Phone numbers
_____	Locations
_____	Subcontractor names, descriptions
_____	Default revenue and expense accounts
_____	Estimate or quotation data

Need Level	Job/Project Tracking (cont.):
	Reports—
_____	Job Ledger Listing
_____	Job Profitability Report
_____	Job Transaction Listings

Payroll:

Need Level	
_____	View/print any employee history
	Employee Master File—
_____	Employee number as well as name
_____	Multiple addresses
_____	Multiple phone numbers
_____	E-mail address
_____	Employee type (hourly, weekly, salary)
_____	Pay rates
_____	Social Security Number
_____	Department
	Company Master File—
_____	Unemployment rate
_____	Special deductions

Pay period activity:

Need Level	
_____	Use time cards
_____	Regular hours separate from overtime
_____	Commissions
_____	Special deductions
_____	Print checks one at a time *or*
_____	Print checks in a batch
_____	Ability to reprint erroneous checks
_____	Distribute payroll to departments
_____	Record employer payroll taxes automatically

Payroll Reports:

Need Level	
_____	Payroll checks
_____	Payroll Journal
_____	Employee Earnings Record
_____	940 Form
_____	941 Form
_____	Quarterly Payroll Summary
_____	W-4 Forms
_____	W-2 Forms

_____	**Your number of employees**

Additional Capabilities

Need Level	
_____	Depreciation calculator
_____	Professional time and billing
_____	Sample company and sample chart of accounts
_____	Import/Export data in all modules
_____	Guided tutorial for startup
_____	Multi-user version (for network use)
_____	Password for full system
_____	Multi-level passwords
_____	Report customization for all components

What Do You Want the Accounting Package to Do for You?

Basic Functions

Figure 2-3 lists the capabilities of the common accounting modules that were presented in Figure 2-1. This is a detailed list of the specific tasks that are performed by each of the major modules in an accounting package. Careful perusal of this list will give you an idea of whether one of the low-end packages can meet your needs. For instance it might be important for you to know if the payroll module tracked vacation and sick time or accommodated deductions for dental insurance.

Determining your needs is the most important preparation for choosing the right software package. Compare your needs with the features of the software packages you are considering buying.

Figure 2-3: *Features commonly found in accounting software packages for under $300*

General Ledger (GL)	**Accounts Payable** (AP)	Integration with Inventory
Sample Chart of Accounts	Vendor master file	View/print Vendor Ledger for
Up to 7 digit account numbers	Pop-up vendor file during	all or a specific vendor
Sublevels within each account	data entry	Standard AP reports
(to handle departments/div)	Pop-up Chart of Accounts	Mailing labels
Pop-up Chart of Accounts	during data entry	
during data entry	Default GL accounts	**Accounts Receivable** (AR)
General Journal entries	Enter vendors on the fly	Customer master file
Recurring transactions	Purchase Orders (PO)	Pop-up customer file during
Adjustments to prior periods	POs converted to Invoices	data entry
Automatic reversing entries	Calculate discounts	Default GL accounts entered
Budgets for GL accounts	Distribute costs to jobs	on transactions
Budget comparison to actual	Apply reimbursable costs to	Enter customers on-the-fly
Budget comparison to last year	customers	Quotes convert to invoices
General ledger audit trail	Returns and Allowances	Invoice customization
each period	Payments against invoices	Calculates discounts & finance
General ledger view/print for	Payments without invoices	charges
a specific account	Partial payments	Distribute revenue to jobs
Trial Balance any time	Batch check printing	Charge reimbursable costs
Month-end closing procedure	Void checks	to customers
Year-end closing procedure	Recurring payments	Recurring transactions
Data export capability	1099 vendors/year-end forms	Returns and allowances
Financial Statements—	Correct errors easily	Receipts on account
Income Statement (Profit	Project cash requirements	Bank deposit slips
and Loss)	Cash Disbursements Journal	Partial payments
Balance Sheet	Purchases Journal	Customer Statements
Statement of Cash Flows		

Figure 2-3 cont.

View/print Customer Ledger for all or a specific customer
Easy error correction
Invoice Register
Sales Journal
Cash Receipts Journal
Aged Receivables Report
Integration with inventory system
Standard AR reports
Mailing labels

Payroll
Employee master file
Company master deductions file
Federal Tax Tables
State Tax Tables for every state
Employees in several states
Pop-up employee lest during data entry
Default GL accounts for each employee
Calculates and deducts federal and state withholding, FICA, local taxes
Recalls previous period pay
Unlimited custom deductions
Batch check printing
Payroll Register Easy error correction
Detailed earnings history by employee
Federal tax forms: W-4, W-2, 941, 940, etc.

Track vacation & sick time
Pay weekly, bi-weekly, semi-monthly, or monthly
Hourly, salaried, and tipped employees
Distribute wages to jobs
Workers compensation reports
Standard payroll reports
Tax table updates each year

Inventory
Integration with General Ledger, Accounts Payable, Payroll, and Accounts Receivable
Inventory master file
Alpha or numeric inventory IDs
Automatic item pricing by per-cent, markup, or margin basis
Pop-up inventory file during data entry in other modules
Non-stock/description only items
Adjustments Journal
Calculates cost of sales
View/print inventory ledger for all or specific item
Sales activity by inventory item
Choice of inventory costing method
Reorder quantity on file
Reorder Report
Standard Inventory Reports

Job/Project Tracking
Track costs and revenue to jobs or projects
Integrated with General Ledger, Accounts Payable, Payroll, and Accounts
Job/project master file
Alpha or numeric job IDs
Pop-up job/project file during data entry
Job start/end dates, quotes, and employee names
View/print job ledger
Standard job/project reports

Other
Password protection
Bank reconciliation
Depreciation calculator
Professional time billing
Loan amortization
To do lists
Data import/export
Report customization
Getting started guided tour
Easy to use, context-based help
Built in backup procedure
Intuitive menus/icon bar
Detailed user manual
Customer support phone line

Comparing Your Needs to What Is Available

On your marked-up photocopy of the Figure 2-2 needs checklist, highlight the items that you identified as required (R) for your business. Using a different color, highlight the items you marked as desirable (D). Then take the needs checklist and place a check mark next to each of your highlighted items that seems to be covered by the features list of Figure 2-3. If all your needs are taken care of by the features list, you probably will do very well to start with Peachtree, QuickBooks, One-Write Plus, or one of the other top ten software packages.

If some of your needs are not covered by the features list, then you should explore the power of the package that most closely fits your specifications by calling the customer service phone number of the software vendor (see Appendix A) to ask them specifically how their accounting package handles your unique need. If you find that quite a few of your needs are not matched by the features list of Figure 2-3, you might need to explore full-featured software as described in Chapter 1.

One other level of need that you should verify is the volume of transactions you will need to handle. Notice that in Figure 2-2, there are lines for estimating the number of your vendors, customers, employees, and inventory items. If you have fewer than two hundred customers, two hundred vendors, and one thousand inventory items, the low-end category of software should serve you adequately. If your needs exceed these numbers, you should verify with a vendor that their software will handle your volume of transactions.

Prioritizing Your Needs

Unless you have an intuitive feel for the priority level of the needs you listed using Figure 2-2, you will be a wiser shopper if you revisit your needs list to assign priorities to the required items. Place a 1, 2, or 3 next to each of your required items, using the number 1 for most important. For example, if Inventory is your top priority, put a big 1 next to the Inventory section; then within the Inventory category put a 1 next to fields that you must have in your inventory item file. For instance, you may put a 1 next to Price List, and/or Automatic Purchase Orders for Inventory Reordering, but a 3 next to the ability to view item history, even though all are required items.

Getting the Details on a Specific Package

The next step is to discover if the packages you have identified as good candidates can efficiently do all those things that are your highest priorities. Call the vendors, or go to your local computer store, and request a specifications sheet for each of those prospective packages. A sample specifications sheet for M.Y.O.B. is shown in Figure 2-4. Take a look at the features under Inventory and Purchases & Payables. With this type of specifications list, you should be able to get a clearer picture of how that specific software package matches up with your needs checklist.

Figure 2-4: *Sample specifications list for M.Y.O.B.*

General Ledger
At last, a general ledger that lets you correct mistakes!
- 100 starter Charts of Accounts
- Step-by-step general ledger setup
- Up to 26 accounting periods can remain open — no need to close out months!
- 4 levels of detail in chart of accounts
- Complete analysis of balance sheet and P&L
- Integrated job profit and loss tracking
- Current year vs. last year comparisons
- Traceable transaction history
- Transactions can be changed or automatically reversed

Checkbook
Deposits and withdrawals produced automatically!
- Checks look and work like your paper checks
- Bank statement reconciliation is a simple matter of making the "X" mark the spot
- Recurring checks and deposits feature does your banking for you
- Powerful cash flow worksheet gives you a financial overview
- Customizable checks and stubs let you design your own look
- Cash flow analysis instantly available

Sales
Flexibility and freedom!
- Variable credit terms per customer or per invoice
- Credit memos produced
- Customizable invoices and statements
- Four standard invoice formats: service, item, professional and other
- Returns and adjustments handled easily
- Sales analysis, including charts and graphs
- Instant receivables analysis
- Recurring and pending invoices
- Quickly and easily handles estimates and quotes

Payroll (Optional)
Finally, a payroll system so easy to use, there's no reason not to!
- Easy setup includes predefined income, deduction, accruals, and employer expenses—or lets you define your own!
- Handles hourly, salary and non-cash wages
- Automatic calculation of payroll taxes
- Printable W2s and 1099s
- Real-time update to balance sheet and P&L statement
- Virtually limitless wage, deduction and accrual categories
- Sixteen payroll reports
- Fully integrated with the rest of the program
- Vacation and sick pay accrual on pay stub

Purchases
Buying is quick and easy!
- Tracks purchases and payables
- Handles returns and debit memos
- Calculates discounts
- Includes recurring and pending purchase orders
- Contains reports by vendor or item
- Produces payables reconciliation report

Inventory
Functional and friendly!
- Builds finished goods from raw materials
- Backorders goods automatically
- Flags low inventory
- Prices items by % or amount automatically
- Calculates average inventory cost
- Reports inventory on hand

Card File
No more forget-me-nots!
- Remembers names, addresses and phone numbers for easy contacts
- Identifies specific groups of your customers and vendors for mail merge
- Keeps an on-going contact log summary of your notes
- Generates mailing labels
- Includes a powerful search function

M.Y.O.B. Analyst
Instant financial and management information!
- Performance to date analysis and graphs
- Provides instant access to critical financial information, including sales, payables and inventory analysis
- Records money owed and money due
- Reminds you of expiring discounts

Selection Factors

Besides identifying your business needs, there are a few other factors that you should pay close attention to when selecting accounting software.

Vendor Reputation

The software vendor I have been talking about is the company that holds the license to sell (and that probably developed) the accounting software package. For example, Intuit, Inc., is the vendor for QuickBooks, and Peachtree is the vendor for One-Write Plus and Peachtree for Windows. Ask around about the vendor's reputation for customer support. A good vendor will offer a minimum of thirty to sixty days of free phone support after the sale (or upgrade); later expect to pay by the minute for advice or be ready to sign an annual contract for unlimited support. Most accounting software vendors do not have toll-free telephone numbers for technical support, but when you call their help line, you should get to talk to a friendly human immediately, without wading through minutes of instructions about what number to press to get help. Good customer support starts with a friendly voice and a response that gives you confidence that the helper knows your software intimately. If the answer to your problem isn't immediately forthcoming, the vendor should offer to call you back within the hour. Go ahead, make a test call to the "help line" of a vendor you are considering. Sample question: "How does this package handle finance charges on overdue accounts receivables, and where do I find this on a menu?"

If a software vendor provides an electronic bulletin board or a Web site for posting questions and receiving answers, has a technical support e-mail address, offers technical support by fax, mails a newsletter full of tips, directs you to local user groups, or even has a section of their user's manual devoted to "how to contact the customer support department," then it is trying to offer good support. If you can't determine if a vendor has any of the above, you should be wary, but you may have alternative sources of help. Does your software store offer help? Can you find a local user group? References about vendor or other support from current users of the package are invaluable if your source of information is not appreciably more computer-savvy than you.

Intuit Corporation (vendor for QuickBooks) sponsors a telephone system called the User Group Locator. Call 914-876-6678 to find out the names and phone numbers of a computer user group in your state. User Groups are highly tuned organizations of PC users who like to get together to talk about issues and new opportunities in the computer world. Many User Groups have subgroups that are specifically concerned with accounting. Once you get the name of a local group, call them to ask about their special interest groups and meeting dates and topics. The User Group Locator is not just for Intuit customers—anyone can call it.

Test Drives

There is absolutely no better way to find out what an accounting package is like than to "test drive" it yourself. Search out all possibilities for this. Your local computer store or a CPA firm that sells software might have a copy available on a demo computer for you to try. The Small Business Development Center (SBDC), part of the federal government's Small Business Administration, in my city has QuickBooks and One-Write Plus available for anyone to try out. The national office of the SBA (address in the Appendix) can point you toward a local office. Another businessperson in your area who owns the package in which you are interested might agree to do a demo for you, as might an accounting professor who teaches accounting software.

What should you look for? Browse the user's manual to see if it is easy to read. Are topics listed where you expect to find them? Is the software user friendly for you? If there is a tutorial, take the time to try it out. Tutorials usually have a sample company provided—play around with a few transactions. If you have permission to store some files, choose a default chart of accounts, set up your own company, enter a few customers and vendors, and then try out a few transactions. Print the reports that you are most likely to want for your business. Did the package easily perform your highest-priority items from Figure 2–2? Was the on-screen help useful?

Sources of Information

You've read of several sources of information about accounting software in the previous paragraphs. Let me summarize the ones I have mentioned and add a few more:

- local computer user groups, ask if they have an accounting or financial software group (See the Appendix for phone numbers and addresses)
- electronic forums on the Internet for a specific software package (e.g., CompuServe sponsors a forum on One-Write Plus)
- vendor sales lines (usually toll-free); vendor help lines (usually not toll-free)
- World Wide Web home pages of the software vendors (e.g., www.peach.com or www.intuit.com)
- software vendor's newsletter; suggest they start one if they don't already have one
- a local business using the software you are interested in or own
- commercial accounting software evaluators, e.g., CTS, Inc., publishes *Guide to Small Business Accounting Software, Guide to Software for the Construction Industry*, etc. (check your local or college library, bookstore, or software store)

- computer and/or accounting magazines and journals such as *Accounting Technology* (Faulkner & Gray Publishers), *Small Business Computing*, or *Home Office Computing*
- continuing or adult education courses on accounting software
- your local SBA office, SBDC (Small Business Development Center), and state or regional Economic Development Offices
- the CPA association in your state might give you a list of local accountants who specialize in accounting software
- local college and university accounting professors who teach courses on computerized accounting
- small business conferences and workshops usually include sessions and exhibitors for accounting software
- your librarian and/or the librarian at the nearest college
- Yellow Pages under accountants for those who help small businesses set up their accounting systems

In your search, be sure the information you get is at an accounting and computer-understanding level that is best for you. Also be aware that some people who have information can't always teach it. Choose your sources carefully.

The Implementation Process

Well, congratulations! You've gotten yourself an accounting software package. Now you need a strategy for installing the software on your computer and making it work for you. This process is called the implementation stage.

Installation

Before loading any new program on your computer, backup all your current data. You should be doing this regularly anyway.

The process of actually loading the software onto your hard disk and signifying the printer type, monitor, etc. has become relatively pain-free. Software vendors have worked hard to automate the installation process. After you answer a few questions, like the type of company you operate, whether you want accrual or cash basis accounting, and how many accounting periods you want to have in a year, the software does the rest. It copies files from diskettes or CD-ROM to your hard disk and sets up beginning data files for your company. Peachtree, for example, sets up one file for your general ledger accounts, another for your customers, another for your vendors, etc.

Play Time

Most accounting packages come with a tutorial or at least a getting started guided tour. Try them! You don't have to proceed through the whole set of lessons or demonstrations—quit at any time, then go back when you need to learn something new. The guided tours usually give you a good overview of procedures and can smooth the way for your own startup. For example, QuickTour from QuickBooks made me aware of the power of the graphing capability that was not available in the earlier versions of QuickBooks for DOS. Figure 2-5 provides a screen view of the graphs section of the QuickTour.

Figure 2–5: *Screen from QuickBooks tour of new features*

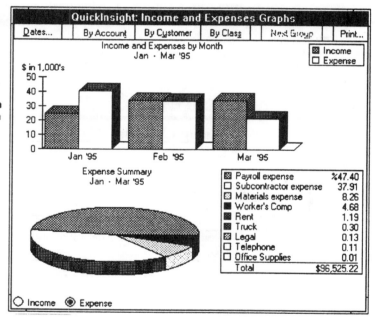

QuickBooks gives you insight into your business with over 60 preset reports and graphs.

QuickZoom lets you see the details behind the numbers. Whenever the mouse pointer turns into a magnifying glass, you can double-click to see more detail.

Click Show me to see how QuickZoom works.

Show me

Books from the Box

The books included in the box with your software are called user's manuals; they are full of helpful descriptions for procedures the software can perform. All right, I realize that no one wants to sit down and read the software user's manual before starting to use their new software. But, really, it might help! Go away from your computer and look over the Table of Contents. Read just a few sections that interest you. If you are most worried about collections and customer relations, then read the section on setting up customer files, writing invoices, and managing customer balances. Choose a time when you will not be interrupted so you can learn and enjoy all your new software is going to do for you. Oh No! There are no books! If your software is one of the new CD versions, all of your help and instructions may be on-screen. The read-me file will tell you how to take advantage of this feature and how to print out the sections that interest you.

Software Setup

Peachtree uses on-screen boxes called SmartGuides to walk you through the steps of the setup procedure. First, you must choose a chart of accounts to use, then enter customer names and addresses, vendor names and addresses, employees, sales tax jurisdictions, sales tax codes and rates, inventory items, and so on (not necessarily in that order). Each module will require that you specify, or verify, some default settings like the accounts receivable account number and the data entry method that you prefer. Peachtree provides a Setup Checklist (see Figure 2-6) where you point-and-click to place a check mark next to the setup tasks you have completed, so you will know what is still left to be done. This is an especially helpful feature. Read the Setup Checklist in Figure 2-6 to get a feel for the scope of this stage of the implementation process.

Figure 2-6: *Setup checklist from Peachtree*

		Setup Checklist
		General Ledger
	▶	Enter general ledger default settings
✓	▶	Enter general ledger chart of accounts
✓	▶	Enter general ledger account beginning balances
		Accounts Receivable
✓	▶	Enter customer default settings
	▶	Enter statement/invoice default settings
✓	▶	Enter customer records
	▶	Enter customer beginning balances
		Accounts Payable
✓	▶	Enter vendor default settings
	▶	Enter vendor records
	▶	Enter vendor beginning balances
		Payroll
✓	▶	Enter employee default settings
	▶	Enter employee records
	▶	Enter employee year-to-date earnings and withholdings
		Inventory
	▶	Enter inventory default settings
✓	▶	Enter inventory items and assemblies
	▶	Enter inventory beginning quantities
		Jobs
	▶	Enter jobs default settings
	▶	Enter jobs
	▶	Enter job beginning balances

HELP, F1, Help!, ? (On-screen Assistance)

Every software package—accounting or otherwise—provides a built-in help system whereby you press a key (usually the F1 key) or click a word (Help or a ? mark) and you open a "book" full of reference information. This is the software's help system. If a package provides context-sensitive help, it means that you will be shown help on whatever task you were performing at the time you summoned the help. For example, if you were in the process of specifying the selling terms when you were adding customers to your customer master file and then clicked on the menu word "help," you would be shown information on what "selling terms" means, with examples of the most common selling terms.

No matter where you are in the help system, you should be able to see an "index" and a "search" menu item or icon. When you choose the index option, you will see a list of the letters of the alphabet. Clicking on any letter brings you to a list of topics that start with that letter. Drill down further by choosing a topic from the index. The search option lets you type a few letters or words from any topic that you are looking for, and the software will search all help files for any occurrence of the letters or phrase you specified. You can always move back to the previous Help screen by clicking on a "back" icon (it is sometimes in symbol form, like << for "back").

Figure 2-7 shows the table of contents from the One-Write Plus help system. As you point to any item, you will see a small hand appear over that item (here the hand is on "customers & sales"). Double click on your topic and the "book" will open to the section on that topic.

Figure 2-7: *Sample from One-Write Plus system*

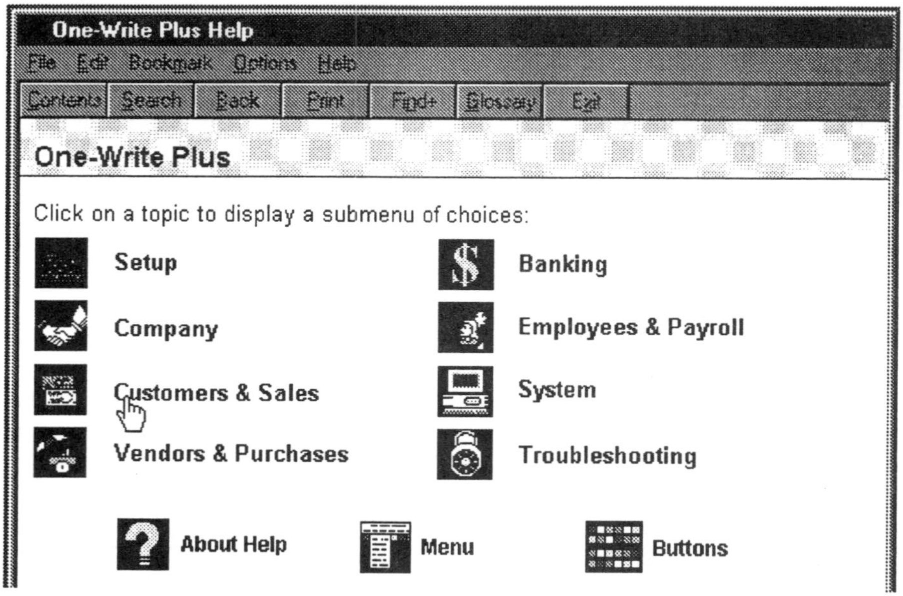

Data Entry

No one can avoid the rather tedious keyboarding task of initially entering records in the basic accounting master files. Basic startup data includes the customer and vendor names. If you are not a new business, you also need to enter beginning balances in those customer and vendor accounts, as well as the accounts in your general ledger, payroll, and inventory files. If you return to Figure 2-6 you will notice that each section includes an item for entering the basic records of that module and entering beginning balances for those records. Good screen prompts, easy movement around the screen fields, and automatic fill-in of repetitive fields can really help during this stage. For example, look for a program that automatically displays the city, state, and zip code of the previous customer so you can accept those items or type over them. This can really be a time saver if most of your customers are in Portland, ME, at zip codes 04102 and 04103! After each hour you invest in data entry, be sure you make a backup copy of your files (read the "backup" section later in this chapter). Each hour is a minimum; you may choose to backup more often.

Verification with Old System

Wise computer users test to see if the new computer system is working correctly by using "parallel runs." They continue to do their accounting the old way (manually or with the old software) for a few months while also doing all the record keeping with the new accounting software package. You should at least overlap by a month. This might require hiring a typist from a temporary employment agency, but it will be worth it. Make sure the total of your accounts payable, accounts receivable, and employee earnings records is the same with your old system as it is on your new software. Run an income statement from both the old and the new for at least that one month period to be sure they are the same.

Troubleshooting

There is probably no such thing as a trouble free conversion from an old accounting system to a new one. Here are just some of the things that might go wrong and some hints on how to deal with them.

If your new income statement does not match your old one: match them side by side to see which accounts are off. If revenue accounts are wrong, run a sales journal from both systems to look at each transaction that went into revenue. If expense accounts are off, run a cash disbursements journal and purchases journal from both systems and compare them.

If your accounts receivable or payable balances don't match between the "old" way and the "new" way, determine which customers are off and match the transaction detail within those accounts. You might have to print a full transaction journal or register from both systems to discover the discrepancies. Once you identify an item that caused a difference (discrepancy) you will decide whether to change your old system or your new system.

Be aware that your decision to switch from cash to accrual basis or LIFO to FIFO inventory may render a comparison impossible.

If no reports print from your new software, check to see if there is a "preferences" or "system defaults" item on any of your menus. This may be where you specify what printer you are using. With Windows software, the problem is often with the Windows Print Manager. The Print Manager always tries to take control of print jobs, but the software may also be trying to control that job. Look for a "printer problems" section in the Help system and the user's manual.

A Few Tricks

Some commonsense advice: spend a lot of time looking at and refining the chart of accounts that appears after you have chosen one of the sample charts. Read more about the chart of accounts in Chapter 3 if you are not familiar with this very important tool. You will probably want to delete some accounts and add others. Take the time to do this up front because it helps you get to know that chart of accounts better and could help you avoid omissions that will cause problems later. For example, you might want to separate current assets into "cash" items and "tangible items."

On the subject of data entry—look for every shortcut you can find! Don't assume that you have to type in every character. For example, most packages will allow you to enter a month and day and leave off the year; the software will provide the current year. Just type "7/2", and QuickBooks will make that "07/02/97" and even display it as July 2, 1997 in some places. You can often press "+" and "-" to increment the date by one day forward or back. Find out if your software will allow you to repeat data in a field based on what you used in the last entry. For example, when entering multiple inventory items that have a unit measure of "gallon" or "pint," you should be able to press ENTER or TAB to repeat the last data used for that field. Read the "shortcut keys" section of your Help system and user's manual to find other quick ways to automate data entry.

The next most important thing to understand about your new system is how it saves data. It should be fairly automatic, but you don't want to be surprised to find that the first three invoices you entered have disappeared because you clicked "next" on a toolbar instead of using "post." Some software doesn't include a "save" menu item or icon because the transaction is saved automatically as it is posted; or better yet, when you exit from the data entry screen it informs you that it will SAVE unless you say "No." And speaking of saving—an important act of saving is the saving of backup copies. Those are copies of your company files that are saved on diskettes or magnetic tape. Here's how you do it.

Backing Up Your Files

The process of backing up your accounting data is so important that it will be mentioned many times in this book. You spend a lot of time creating your accounting records, and they provide you with critical decision making power; it will be a disaster if you lose them. To guard against a loss of control and service because of computer system failure, you must prepare backup copies of your accounting data on a regular basis!!!

All businesses should develop a procedure for making backup copies of accounting data every time new data is entered—usually on a daily basis. Put this procedure in writing and follow it! It is recommended that five sets of backup diskettes be maintained—disks are cheap compared to the value of your time or the cost of losing your data. For example, use set #1 on Monday, set #2 on Tuesday, set #3 on Wednesday, set #4 on Thursday, and set #5 on Friday. Then overwrite set #1 on the following Monday, overwrite set #2 next Tuesday, and so forth. Each time you use a backup disk, the date of the backup should be penciled on the diskette label. Every other day the backup data set should be stored in a location physically removed from the computer—in a fireproof safe or at off-site storage. You won't appreciate the importance of this until you or a friend suffers a fire, flood, earthquake, theft, or other disaster.

In Peachtree, QuickBooks, and One-Write Plus, you will find the "backup" command on the File menu. QuickBooks considers this procedure to be so important that there is an icon on the toolbar labeled "backup" (see Figure 1-1). Find the backup command for your software, and use it religiously! If your backup files will not fit on a single diskette and/or the process takes more than fifteen minutes, you should seriously consider a larger capacity storage device like magnetic tape.

Here is an example of how the backup procedure works. When you select the "file, backup" commands in Peachtree, the window in Figure 2-8 appears. If you accept the defaults shown in this window, a second set of files for all your accounting data will be placed in a subdirectory within your company directory under the "PEACHW" directory of your hard disk drive with the name of "BAK." In other words, the backup files will be stored in C:\peachw\yourco\bak. If you want to store your backup files on a diskette in the A: disk drive, which I highly recommend, simply type A: in place of the "BAK" that is showing in the destination box. Peachtree provides the option of using a simple "copy" (for small companies) or a "DOS backup" (for larger companies whose files will not fit all on one disk). Don't worry—choose the simple "copy" at first, and when your files get too big for that method, the computer will inform you to try the other option. Other accounting software handles the backup routine in a similar way. Check your user's manual for more information on making backup copies and what to do if you ever need to use those backups.

Figure 2-8: *Backup options window from Peachtree*

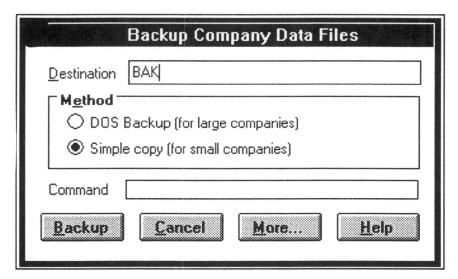

A Few Last Words

It is rare to find the perfect accounting package that fills all your needs. Expect to compromise a bit; expect to modify your procedures a little. Use of the ideas in this chapter should help you make good decisions on these matters. Don't wait for better options; take the plunge or you will fall behind your braver competitors. It is surely acceptable to adopt an accounting package simply because your accountant is familiar with it or a friend uses it; this way you will have an experienced user nearby. I strongly recommend that you read about the general ledger in Chapter 3 if you are installing accounting software for the first time.

Chapter Three

General Ledger Accounting

Introduction to the General Ledger

The general ledger (GL) is the place where all accounting ends up (it is the end-product), but we need to study it first in order to prepare for understanding how an accounts payable or accounts receivable module integrates into the GL. The GL is the set of accounts that a business has identified as the financial items that it wants to track. For example, the GL contains an account for cash, an account for inventory, an account for notes payable, an account for owner equity, an account for revenue, an account for advertising expense, and so forth.

The general ledger, a set of accounts, is named in a document called the chart of accounts. These accounts are used to collect data as transactions occur in your daily operations. The data is accumulated (added to or subtracted from the ongoing balances in the accounts) and reported periodically so that the business owners and managers can see how profitable the business has been over a period of time, to determine what kind of financial shape the business is in, and to guide management decisions.

This chapter presents a detailed description of how a general ledger works and how it relates to the other parts of an accounting system.

Introduction to Accounting Principles

The accounting profession has, over the years, developed a set of rules for recording financial transactions that are called the generally accepted accounting principles (GAAP). These principles range from the time-tested method of using a balancing act called double-entry bookkeeping (with debits and credits), to the more obscure rules of depreciation and amortization. When I refer to accounting principles in this book, I am referring to these principles developed by accountants in industry, nonprofit organizations, academia, and private practice. The general principles are the same for all businesses, and these same principles were used in the design of Peachtree, QuickBooks, One-Write Plus, and other small business accounting software. Some of the most important principles follow.

Business Entity Concept

The rule that a business organization is treated as a separate and distinct legal entity is the business entity concept. This business entity enters into contracts, sells its name and services, and generally operates as an organization that is separate and distinct from its owners. In keeping with this concept, the records of the business must be totally separate from the records of the owners.

Basic Components: Assets, Liabilities, and Equity

In order for prospective investors and current owners to have confidence in a set of financial records, there must be built in controls. The most important aspect of this control is the idea that the entire collection of accounts in a set of records be broken down into three basic categories with those categories always being in balance with one another. Those categories are the assets, the liabilities, and the owner equity in the business. They remain in balance with each other by adherence to the basic accounting equation:

$$\text{Assets} = \text{Liabilities} + \text{Owner Equity}$$

Assets are things of value that the business owns like cash, inventory, and equipment.

Liabilities are debts that the business owes, like notes payable, accounts payable, and taxes payable.

Owner Equity is the sum of all owner investments, enriched by revenue earned and eroded by expenses and/or owner withdrawals. (In a corporation, the owner investments are called "paid in capital" or "capital stock" and the withdrawals are made in the form of "dividends.")

The general ledger is the organized collection of the accounts in each of these three categories. We will later discuss how these basic categories are the ingredients of a balance sheet and how this report presents the balanced proof of the equation: Assets = Liabilities + Owner Equity.

How Transactions Affect Assets, Liabilities, and Owner Equity

Each business transaction will affect the basic accounting equation by having a dual effect—that is, the transaction will be recorded by having two "sides," a debit (left) side and a credit (right) side. I'll explain debits and credits in a few minutes, but for now, just think of the basic equation as being an algebraic equation that must always remain in balance. When the owner invests $5,000 cash to start a business, the equation goes from being $0 = $0 to

Assets	=	Liabilities	+	Owner Equity
Cash $5000 =		$0	+	Capital $5,000

Cash is an asset and the original owner's investment is recorded as owner capital. Each of these categories increases by the same amount, keeping the overall equation in balance, now at $5,000 = $5,000. When the business borrows $3,000 cash from the bank, its cash goes up and its liabilities increase by $3,000. The accounting equation goes from $5,000 = $5,000 to

Assets	=	Liabilities	+	Owner Equity
Cash $8000 =		Notes $3,000	+	Capital $5,000

Notes payable is a liability that increases the total liabilities by $3,000 and the cash borrowed increases the assets, cash, by $3,000. The basic equation of "assets = liabilities + owner equity" remains in balance at $8,000 = $8,000. If the business then used $1,000 of its cash to buy equipment, it gains a new asset, equipment, in trade for the old asset, cash. This takes us from $8,000 = $8,000 to

Assets		=	Liabilities	+	Owner Equity
Cash	$7,000				
Equipment	$1,000	=	Notes $3,000	+	Capital $5,000

At this point the equation is still in balance at $8,000 = $8,000 because this last transaction caused an increase in one asset (equipment) and a decrease in another asset (cash), but had no effect on liabilities or owner equity.

Handling Revenue and Expenses

Lastly, it is important to understand that revenue and expenses are considered to be subcategories of owner equity. Think of it this way: net profit is determined by subtracting expenses from revenue. Net profit increases the owner's equity (it improves your investment in the business), while a net loss decreases owner equity. Using the balances from the last example ($8,000 = $8,000) let's factor in some revenue and expenses. When this hypothetical business finishes a customer job billed at $2,000 and collects the cash immediately, the transaction affects the equation like this:

Assets		=	Liabilities	+	Owner Equity
Cash	$9,000				Capital $5,000
Equipment	$1,000 =		Notes $3,000	+	Revenue $2,000
Totals:	$10,000 =				$10,000

As you can see, the cash account is increased by $2,000 and the revenue (or owner equity) account is increased by $2,000. Each side of the equation is increased by the same amount, with the totals being $10,000 = $10,000. When an expense of $1,500 is paid in cash, the equation is affected as follows:

Assets		=	Liabilities	+	Owner Equity
Cash	$7,500				Capital $5,000
Equipment	$1,000 =		Notes $3,000	+	Revenue $2,000
					Expense ($1,500)
Totals:	$8,500 =				$8,500

Assets (cash) are decreased by $1,500 and owner equity (for an expense) is decreased by $1,500 still keeping the equation in balance at $8,500 = $8,500.

Although the above is simplistic, and much briefer than presentations in accounting books, it provides you with an understanding of the basic foundation of accounting. There are just a few more simple accounting principles that will enhance the picture of how accounting software works.

Accrual Basis vs. Cash Basis

The accrual basis of accounting provides a much more accurate picture of your profit but requires the recording of all credit transactions and adjustments like depreciation. It is acceptable for a company to choose between maintaining their accounting records on a cash basis or on an accrual basis. If you choose the cash basis, this means that you will only record revenue and expense transactions when cash changes hands—not when a shipment is received or when goods or services are delivered to the customer. If you choose the accrual basis, you will record revenue when it is earned (when the goods are shipped or the service is performed) and record expenses when they are incurred (when you receive goods or services, or are bound by an obligation to pay), whether cash changes hands or not.

The accrual basis of accounting allows you to get a more accurate picture of your net profit (revenue minus expenses) because the revenue reflects all the work you have done in a period, even though some of the money for the work is in accounts receivable, and the expenses include all the obligations you have entered into in order to earn that revenue, even though some of the payments are being delayed as payables.

Here is an example of thinking on the accrual basis. The company automobile is repaired on May 10, and you receive an invoice that is due in thirty days. You would record this on May 10 as an increase in automobile maintenance expense and as an increase in accounts payable. Your May net profit would then reflect the true cost (expense) of operating that automobile in May. Thirty days later, June 10, you would pay that invoice. Your software will decrease cash by the invoice amount and decrease accounts payable by the same amount. The auto-mobile expense is truly a May expense, not a June expense.

GAAP recommends the use of the accrual method, so I will assume use of the accrual method in this book.

Cash Basis Choice with Accounting Software

If you want to maintain your records on a cash basis, you may specify this in most modern accounting packages, then you may still maintain a customer ledger and/or vendor ledger. Using the cash basis, sales on account will be recorded in the customer ledger, but the transaction will not be copied (posted) to the revenue and asset accounts. That sale transaction will only be recorded as revenue and cash when the cash is received from the customer. Accounts payable items would be handled in a similar fashion.

Debit/Credit System

In order to keep the assets, liabilities, and equity in balance, debits and credits are used to record each financial transaction. An account is easily illustrated by presenting it in the form of the letter "T." Accountants have been using T-shaped accounts for a couple hundred years.

The way this system works is really quite simple. A "debit" is an addition to an expense or asset account or a deduction from a revenue, capital, or liability account. It appears on the left side of an account. A "credit" is an addition to a revenue, capital, or liability account or a deduction from an expense or asset account. It appears on the right side of an account. Because assets are on the left of the equal sign in the accounting equation, they increase by debiting them (recording on the left side); likewise, since liabilities and owner equity are on the right side of the equal sign, they are increased by crediting them (recording on the right side). All types of accounts are decreased by making an entry on the opposite side from where they are increased. Assets are decreased by crediting them, while liabilities and equity are decreased by debiting them. for example, remember the $5,000 investment of cash by owner that was used in the previous section on the "basic components?" This is how that transaction would look in the accounts:

CASH	
Left Side **Debit** Increases	Right Side **Credit** Decreases
$5000	

OWNER CAPITAL	
Left Side **Debit** Decreases	Right Side **Credit** Increases
	$5000

Here cash is being increased by debiting it; and capital is being increased by crediting it. The rules of debit and credit are very simple and can be summarized this way:

Assets	=	**Liabilities**	+	**Owner Equity**
Debit to increase		Credit to increase		Credit to increase
Credit to decrease		Debit to decrease		Debit to decrease

Revenue accounts are just like owner equity accounts; they increase by crediting them and decrease by debiting. But since expense accounts are the opposite of revenue, they increase on the opposite side. This can be illustrated as:

Owner Equity:
Revenue—
Credit to Increase
Debit to Decrease

Expenses—
Debit to Increase
Credit to Decrease

Normal sales and purchase transactions cause increases in revenue and expense accounts. In other words, when sales are made, the revenue account is increased or credited. When expenses are incurred, an expense account is increased or debited. Later, when net profit is calculated, the total expenses are deducted from total revenue and the difference (net profit) is added to, or (net loss) subtracted from, owner equity.

If all this seems a little overwhelming, don't be too alarmed. The accounting software takes care of all this debiting and crediting for you in most cases. Infrequently, you may use a General Journal (detailed in Chapter 4) where you must specify a debit and a credit. You are much wiser now for understanding a little bit of the mechanics behind the software. Bear with me on a few more general accounting techniques.

Documents, Journals, and Posting

Sales invoices, purchase invoices, checks, deposit receipts, employee time cards, and other documents that flow through your business as evidence of financial dealings are called source documents. These documents are used to record transactions in your accounting system. Modern accounting software allows you to enter the transaction data on electronic replicas of your paper documents, where old fashioned, paper based accounting systems used journals (long lists in chronological order) to record that same data. These days, most transactions will be entered into the screen fields of invoices, deposit receipts, checks, and payroll time cards—the computer will then take care of transferring the data as debits and credits into cash, accounts payable, accounts receivable, other assets, other payables, revenue, and expense accounts. When data is copied from the input screens to accounts, it is said to be "posted"; that is, it is added to or subtracted from the previous balance in the appropriate account in the general ledger. Because most of the data in an electronic accounting system is recorded on sales, purchases, receipts, and payments forms, very few special entries have to be entered directly into the general ledger. A few of these special entries are covered in a later section of this chapter.

Subsystems of the General Ledger

The sales, purchases, receipts, payments, and payroll entries are recorded in subsystems of the general ledger. Purchases and payments are recorded in an accounts payable system (covered in Chapter 5). Sales and receipts are recorded in an accounts receivable system (covered in Chapter 7). Payroll is recorded in a payroll system (covered in Chapter 9). Purchases and sales transactions feed data into an inventory system (covered in Chapter 11). The results of processing in the accounts payable, receivable, and payroll subsystems are eventually transferred to the general ledger; and your accounting software does this automatically! Every sale or purchase is posted (copied) to at least two general ledger accounts.

You can get a general idea of how the subsystems integrate with the general ledger by referring to Figure 3-1, a flowchart of all input and output for the GL.

How a General Ledger System Works

Input

The input, processing, and output of a general ledger is summarized by the flowchart shown in Figure 3-1. You can see from this figure that the major portion of input for the GL comes from the accounts receivable (sales, cash receipts), payable (purchases, cash payments), and payroll subsystems. A few entries are made in a journal called the general journal. The major processing that takes place is the posting to accounts, calculation of new balances in accounts, and a lot of sorting and summarizing to organize the results into useful groups with totals. The output is comprised of the financial statements and several general ledger reports.

Figure 3-1: *General Ledger (GL) data flow diagram*

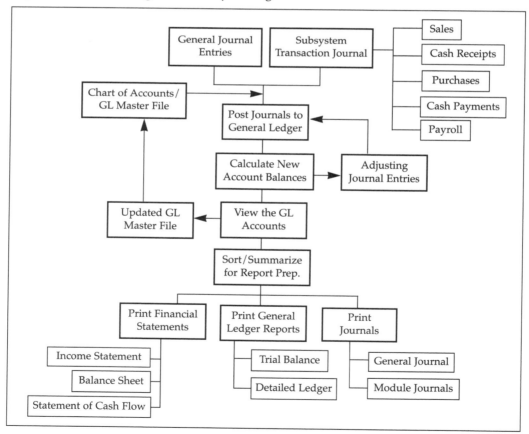

Let's take a closer look at the flow of data and output here. The most common input files and documents for the GL system are:

- the chart of accounts—this is the GL master file
- the transactions from accounts payable (purchases and payments)
- the transactions from accounts receivable (sales and receipts)
- the transactions from payroll
- the transactions from other subsystems requiring posting to GL
- general journal entries (for adjustments & corrections)

The most important input for a GL is the chart of accounts master file, which contains a set of accounts and all data associated with those accounts. Most computer systems, like Peachtree for Windows, are designed so data for accounts payable, accounts receivable, and payroll are entered automatically as purchases, sales, receipts, and checks. If you have your payroll done by an outside payroll service, you receive weekly or monthly reports from them with totals that can be used in a payroll entry in your general journal. The general journal is also used to record normal end of period adjustments like depreciation expense and to correct errors like inadvertently charging advertising expense when you meant to charge automobile expense.

Processing

The basic processing that occurs within a GL system includes:

- the posting (copying) of amounts to general ledger accounts
- the calculation of new balances in accounts
- the display of account history
- the sorting and summarizing of accounts for reports

As described previously, all of the transactions input to the GL must be posted (copied) into accounts, and these transactions are added to or subtracted from previous balances. All of this processing occurs automatically, with the exception of user inquiry of account history. When you want to analyze activity in a specific account (e.g., advertising expense), you are able to easily display all history for just one account. Most importantly, the accounts may be sorted and summarized (group totals) in many ways to accommodate the output reports desired by you.

Output

The most common outputs from a GL system are:

- the transaction journal (general journal)
- the trial balance
- the general ledger account detail
- the financial statements

The only journal normally output by a GL is the general journal. This is a chronological list of transactions that were entered directly into the general ledger—described later in this chapter. The trial balance is a list of all the accounts in the GL with their ending balances. This report not only gives you a bird's-eye view of your accounting records, it proves that the ledger is in balance with the total of debit balance accounts equaling the total of credit balance accounts. The income statement, balance sheet, and statement of cash flows comprise the most common financial statements. These reports are detailed further in Chapter 4.

The Chart of Accounts

A master file is the basic set of fairly permanent information about financial statement categories, or vendors, or customers, or employees that is used repeatedly in the processing of transactions. The chart of accounts master file contains the account names, account numbers, descriptions, and other pertinent information about the required set of accounts that you identify as being necessary for your business.

The most important aspect of setting up a new company with any accounting software is the design of the company chart of accounts. If you don't already have a chart of accounts, this is a topic to discuss with your accountant. All low-end accounting software comes with several sample charts; Peachtree, One-Write Plus, and QuickBooks come with more than ten sample charts for you to choose from. Take a look at Figure 3-2 for a sample chart from Peachtree. You can customize these charts for your business by adding and deleting accounts. (QuickBooks doesn't use a numbering system for accounts—only account names.) Some accounts have been predesignated to be integration accounts (like accounts receivable being account 1200), to be used when entries are automatically posted from the subsystems, so it is usually best to use one of the sample charts provided by the software designers. Figure 3-2 provides a sample chart of accounts for a cleaning service business that includes a few accounts in each of the most common categories.

Figure 3-2: *Sample chart of accounts*

<table>
<tr><td colspan="4" align="center">**Sparkling Cleaning Services**
Chart of Accounts</td></tr>
<tr><th>Account ID</th><th>Account Description</th><th>Active?</th><th>Account Type</th></tr>
<tr><td>1000</td><td>Petty Cash</td><td>Yes</td><td>Cash</td></tr>
<tr><td>1100</td><td>Cash in Savings</td><td>Yes</td><td>Cash</td></tr>
<tr><td>1120</td><td>Cash in Checking</td><td>Yes</td><td>Cash</td></tr>
<tr><td>1200</td><td>Accounts Receivable</td><td>Yes</td><td>Accounts Receivable</td></tr>
<tr><td>1300</td><td>Cleaning Supplies Inventory</td><td>Yes</td><td>Inventory</td></tr>
<tr><td>1320</td><td>Product Inventory</td><td>Yes</td><td>Inventory</td></tr>
<tr><td>1700</td><td>Furniture and Fixtures</td><td>Yes</td><td>Fixed Assets</td></tr>
<tr><td>1710</td><td>Vehicles</td><td>Yes</td><td>Fixed Assets</td></tr>
<tr><td>1720</td><td>Machinery and Equipment</td><td>Yes</td><td>Fixed Assets</td></tr>
<tr><td>1799</td><td>Accumulated Depreciation</td><td>Yes</td><td>Accumulated Depreciation</td></tr>
<tr><td>2000</td><td>Accounts Payable</td><td>Yes</td><td>Accounts Payable</td></tr>
<tr><td>2200</td><td>Notes Payable—Short Term</td><td>Yes</td><td>Other Current Liabilities</td></tr>
<tr><td>2300</td><td>Fed. Payroll W/H Tax—Payable</td><td>Yes</td><td>Other Current Liabilities</td></tr>
<tr><td>2310</td><td>State Payroll W/H Tax—Payable</td><td>Yes</td><td>Other Current Liabilities</td></tr>
<tr><td>2320</td><td>FICA Taxes—Taxes</td><td>Yes</td><td>Other Current Liabilities</td></tr>
<tr><td>2330</td><td>FUTA Taxes—Payable</td><td>Yes</td><td>Other Current Liabilities</td></tr>
<tr><td>2340</td><td>SUTA Taxes—Payable</td><td>Yes</td><td>Other Current Liabilities</td></tr>
<tr><td>2350</td><td>Sales Tax Payable</td><td>Yes</td><td>Other Current Liabilities</td></tr>
<tr><td>2600</td><td>Owners Capital</td><td>Yes</td><td>Equity—Retained Earnings</td></tr>
<tr><td>2800</td><td>Owner's Draw</td><td>Yes</td><td>Equity—gets closed</td></tr>
<tr><td>3000</td><td>Commercial Services Revenues</td><td>Yes</td><td>Income</td></tr>
<tr><td>3100</td><td>Residential Services Revenues</td><td>Yes</td><td>Income</td></tr>
<tr><td>3300</td><td>Interest Income</td><td>Yes</td><td>Income</td></tr>
<tr><td>4000</td><td>Cost of Goods Sold</td><td>Yes</td><td>Cost of Sales</td></tr>
<tr><td>5000</td><td>Salary Expenses</td><td>Yes</td><td>Expenses</td></tr>
<tr><td>5010</td><td>Employer Payroll Tax Expenses</td><td>Yes</td><td>Expenses</td></tr>
<tr><td>5100</td><td>Supplies Expense</td><td>Yes</td><td>Expenses</td></tr>
<tr><td>5200</td><td>Vehicle Expense</td><td>Yes</td><td>Expenses</td></tr>
<tr><td>5550</td><td>Interest Expense</td><td>Yes</td><td>Expenses</td></tr>
<tr><td>5600</td><td>Rent Expense</td><td>Yes</td><td>Expenses</td></tr>
<tr><td>5700</td><td>Insurance Expense</td><td>Yes</td><td>Expenses</td></tr>
<tr><td>5810</td><td>General Office Expenses</td><td>Yes</td><td>Expenses</td></tr>
<tr><td>5820</td><td>Accounting & Legal Expense</td><td>Yes</td><td>Expenses</td></tr>
<tr><td>5830</td><td>Advertising/Marketing</td><td>Yes</td><td>Expenses</td></tr>
<tr><td>5860</td><td>Contract Labor Expense</td><td>Yes</td><td>Expenses</td></tr>
<tr><td>5900</td><td>Utilities Expense</td><td>Yes</td><td>Expenses</td></tr>
<tr><td>5999</td><td>Miscellaneous Expenses</td><td>Yes</td><td>Expenses</td></tr>
<tr><td>6000</td><td>Depreciation Expense</td><td>Yes</td><td>Expenses</td></tr>
</table>

The following are some of the items normally found in a chart of accounts master file:

- account number
- account name
- type of account (asset, liability, revenue, etc.)
- current balance
- financial history for that account
- budget amounts (optional)

Figure 3-3 provides you with a sample screen from Peachtree that is used to add, change, or delete accounts. This master file record contains the above fields for each account that is included in the general ledger. All accounting packages rely on a similar chart of accounts file that is used for the collection of all financial data needed by a business. The data collected in these accounts will become the results reported on your income statement, balance sheet, and statement of cash flows.

Figure 3-3: *Chart of accounts master file record*

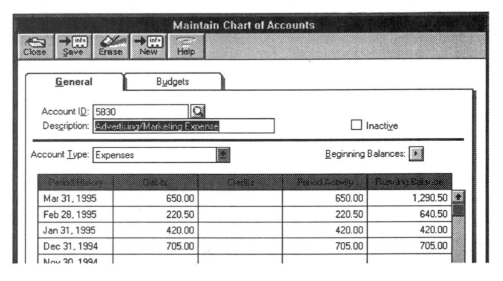

How Software Uses the Chart of Accounts

When a financial transaction is being entered in the general ledger, or in some places in the accounts payable and accounts receivable systems, the data entry screen will require that an account number or name be entered. This account number is the account from the general ledger chart of accounts. The user can access a table of accounts that are already contained in the chart of accounts and select one for the current transaction. Some accounting systems allow you to type the first few characters of an account name or number, and as soon as the computer recognizes the account, it provides the rest of the name and any pertinent items from the master file. For example, in the description field, the user need only type "adv" before the computer would recognize this account as "Advertising/Marketing Expense" and would display the full name and number for that account. Figure 3-4 shows an example of this type of "pop-up" list from Peachtree. If the account being named is not already in the chart of accounts, the computer will notify the user that the account does not exist and encourage the user to enter all necessary data to create a new record in the master file.

Figure 3–4: *Pop-up chart of accounts during data entry*

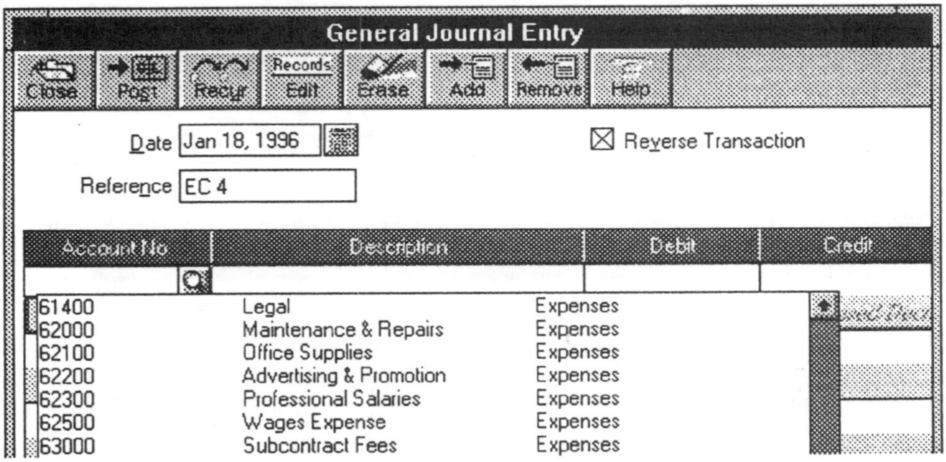

Entering General Ledger Transactions

A comforting thing to know about GL transactions—there are only a very few that will be entered directly in the GL module. Most transactions come from the accounts receivable, accounts payable, and payroll modules, as mentioned previously, and will be covered in detail in the rest of this book. Using the accrual basis of accounting, you will want to make sure that all revenue and expenses that have occurred are actually in the accounts—experienced businesspeople know that this leads to making a few adjustments at the end of the month, such as recording depreciation. These transactions would be recorded in a general journal.

The General Journal

Figure 3-5 illustrates the form of the general journal common to all small business accounting packages. Please notice in this figure that you must provide both the debit and credit—it is not automatic—and that debits must equal credits for each transaction. The example in Figure 3-5 from QuickBooks records depreciation on the company automobile, which in the traditional sense would be recorded as:

		DEBIT	CREDIT
March 15	Depreciation Expense-Truck	$125.	
	Accumulated Depreciation-Truck		$125.

Figure 3-5: *General journal entry screen*

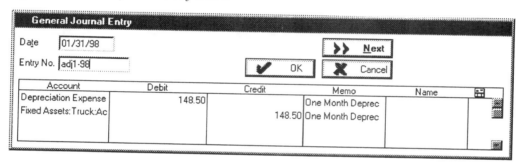

Let's examine the General Journal data entry screen in Figure 3-5. The current date is given as a default date, but the user can overtype any appropriate date. The user then enters an entry number (usually optional). You must then enter (or select from a list) an account number or name to be debited, and the amount to be debited. This is followed by the account number/name, and amount to be credited. An explanation for the entry can also be included (noted as "memo" in this figure). It is possible that you would have several debits and/or credits, but the total of the debit amounts must equal the total of the credit amounts.

The accounting package will include a "post," "save," or "OK" command within its menus or icons. Peachtree offers an icon (or command) to "post" the transaction as seen on the toolbar in Figure 3-4. QuickBooks simply uses an "OK" button seen in the center of Figure 3-5. You can see a "save" icon on the toolbar in Figure 3-6 that is used by One-Write Plus. When this command is executed, the computer will save the transaction and post (copy) it to the accounts named in the entry.

A listing of general journal transactions is normally displayed or printed by producing a listing from the "reports" menu—you can see a sample general journal report in Figure 4-3 of Chapter 4.

Recurring Transactions

Most adjusting entries occur on a repetitive basis—every month or quarter. Some examples are your recorded estimates of monthly depreciation and your procedure for recording interest on bank accounts at the end of each month. In these cases, you know that the journal entry for estimated depreciation or interest income on your money market account must be entered on the last day of every month. In Peachtree, these are known as recurring transactions; QuickBooks and One-Write Plus call them memorized transactions. After a transaction is memorized once, it can be recalled for use whenever you need it in the future.

Here's how it works: While the journal entry of Figure 3-5 is still on screen, you can select the "edit, memorize transaction" menu items in QuickBooks to save copies of the transaction for future use. In One-Write Plus you simply click on the "mem" icon (a little camera) on the toolbar, as seen in Figure 3-6. A dialog box will appear that invites you to specify at what frequency (e.g., once a month, biweekly, quarterly, etc.) that you want the transaction to occur. The transaction will be placed on a list to be used in all future periods that you specified.

When you want to recall a memorized transaction, you ask QuickBooks to retrieve one from "lists, memorized transactions," or click on the "recall" icon in One-Write Plus. Figure 3-6 gives you a peek at a "memorized transaction list" from One-Write Plus, where you simply select the transaction you need, edit it with the current date and amount, and then click "OK" to post it to accounts. No data entry is required in this last step of the process—it's quick and easy!

Figure 3-6: *Sample memorized transaction list*

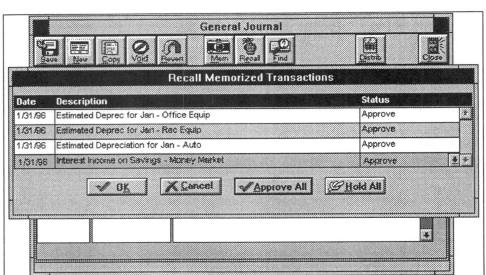

The Trial Balance

When the transactions described in the previous section are posted (copied) into the GL, the account balances in them are updated and new account balances are calculated. The end-result of this work is viewed by producing a trial balance. The trial balance is a list of the ending balances in each account—called a "trial" balance because it should be viewed (on a trial basis) before any financial statements are produced to see that the total of all accounts are balanced between debits and credits. This trial balance proves that the assets equal the total of the liabilities, equity, revenue, and expense accounts. Figure 3-7 provides an example of this GL tool from One-Write Plus, but it will be discussed in more detail in the next chapter.

Figure 3-7: *Sample trial balance*

	Debit	Credit
Jans Jumping Service		
Trial Balance		
As of October 31, 1995		
Checking	34,402.50	
Accounts Payable	6,149.58	
Petty Cash	200.00	
T-Shirts for Sale	8,658.50	
Undeposited Funds	585.00	
Accounts Payable		8,845.50
Sales Tax Payable		86.58
Loan Payable		4,960.00
Owner Equity		30,000.00
Fees		4,885.00
Sales		1,443.00
Services		408.00
Automobile Expense	374.00	
Interest Expense: Loan Interest	146.50	
Maintenance	112.00	
TOTAL	**50,628.08**	**50,628.08**

Account History

The general ledger accounts will contain the detailed history of all transactions—those entered directly into the GL, and those posted (copied) automatically from the accounts receivable, accounts payable, and payroll modules. It is usually not necessary to print all of the history in the GL accounts, but on select occasions, you may want to investigate the history of a specific account. Your accounting software should allow you to "query" any account in the GL (that is, to make a request to see a specific period of history within a specific account). Figure 3-8 provides an example from Peachtree of this query feature—I requested an account history for the advertising expense account for five months so I could get a feel for where we have been spending our advertising dollars. This specialized report can then be printed.

Figure 3-8: *Account history for advertising expense*

Account ID Account Description	Date	Trans Description Jrnl	Debit Amt	Credit Amt	Balance
5830 Advertising/Marketing Exp	1/1/95	Beginning Balance			
	1/5/95	Downing & Assoc. PURJ	420.00		
	2/8/95	Speedy Printer Service PURJ	220.50		
	3/3/95	Speedy Printer Service PURJ	530.00		
	3/3/95	Speedy Printer Service PURJ	120.00		
	5/31/95	**Current Change**	**1,290.50**		**1,290.50**
	5/31/95	**Ending Balance**			**1,290.50**

Bellweather Cleaning Services
General Ledger
For the Period From Jan 1, 1995 to May 31, 1995

Financial Statements

The commonly used financial statements are income statement, balance sheet, and statement of cash flows.

The *income statement* lists the revenue account balances, followed by the expense account balances, with the total expenses subtracted from total revenue to determine net profit (sometimes called net income or net earnings).

The *balance sheet* lists the ending balances in the asset, liability, and owner equity accounts; net income is reported in the owner equity section of the balance sheet so the total of the asset section will equal the sum of the total liabilities plus the owner equity sections.

The *statement of cash flows* uses activity totals from both the income statement accounts and the balance sheet accounts. This statement starts with the beginning period cash balance, shows what cash was received, what cash was paid out, and the ending cash balance.

All of these statements are discussed in detail in the next chapter.

Saving and Backing Up Your Data

The process of backing up your accounting data is so important that it should not be left to chance. All businesses should make backup copies of data files every day! Your software will provide a menu item for this procedure. Develop your own schedule for doing this—but make sure you do it! The procedure for backing up files was illustrated in Chapter 2—"Choosing and Using Accounting Software." If you haven't read that chapter yet, please read "Making Backup Copies."

Conclusion

Are you still with me? Congratulations! This has been a tough chapter to swallow, but you have done your business a tremendous favor by your perseverance with this accounting jargon. You will be able to better control your financial affairs as a result! If you want to get started on the day-to-day tasks of accounting documents, skip to Chapter 5 or 7, but come back before the end of your accounting year to the next important chapter—Chapter 4, "General Ledger Reports."

Chapter Four

General Ledger Reports

Importance of General Ledger Reports

A computerized general ledger (GL) system will produce numerous reports and probably a few graphs. The GL report that you are most interested in is probably the income statement (sometimes called the "Profit and Loss Summary"). The data from the income statement is needed to complete your income tax return. But a General Ledger system will produce many other helpful reports that you will find beneficial once you become more familiar with them. The goal of this chapter is to introduce you to the most common GL reports that are available from your accounting software and to introduce you to some analytical approaches that may help your business become more profitable.

Most modern software provides you with the ability to customize reports to suit your needs. Peachtree for Windows and QuickBooks provide almost unlimited customizing options so you can add or delete rows and columns, change column widths, add or delete totals and subtotals, change font sizes for better readability, and even change the headers/footers on the standard reports provided by the software package. For example, the standard income statement shows the current month and the year-to-date amounts side by side. You can customize that statement to include three months side by side with a quarter total. Let's explore these GL reports.

Getting the Printed Results

Most accounting software packages will have a "reports" icon and/or main menu item labeled "reports." After accessing this reports menu, you may choose from "general ledger, accounts payable, accounts receivable, payroll," etc. One-Write Plus uses the report choices of "financial, banking, customers, vendors," etc. In QuickBooks, some reports are produced using the "reports" menu, but many are produced using the "file, print lists" and "file, print forms" menu commands. When you select "general ledger" (or financial) reports, you will probably be faced with many choices, some of which are:

- balance sheet
- chart of accounts
- general journal
- general ledger (in detail or in summary)
- income statement (in many forms)
- statement of cash flows
- trial balance

Make your choice from the reports list, and you will be allowed to specify some customizing choices like the period of time to include, the heading you prefer, and a host of other options, depending on the sophistication of your accounting package. When you are first experimenting with a new report, just accept the defaults. All accounting software shows reports on screen first (this is a default setting that you can alter if you choose to) and from the displayed report, you click on a "print" icon if you want to send it to paper.

Some of the GL reports are absolutely necessary to the functioning of your business and some you will have to try out to determine if you need them. Let's take a look at the most important of these reports.

Absolutely Necessary Reports

Your printed reports are called the audit trail. Not only will your accountant need this audit trail, but the IRS will require it if it audits you. The GL audit trail includes source documents, such as the note paper you scribbled on when figuring out how much depreciation you wanted to record each month, but more importantly, it includes the printed lists that shows how your accounts have changed each month, quarter, or year. For example, the detailed general ledger printout provides the "trail" that can be used to trace the purpose of each amount back to a specific sales/purchase transaction or even to the original invoice.

At the very least, the GL audit trail should include:

- a detailed general ledger listing
- the income statement and the balance sheet
- a general journal report (if you have entered any general journal entries in the current period)

Chart of Accounts

The chart of accounts was discussed pretty thoroughly in Chapter 3. The important point to keep in mind is that the chart of accounts is a GL list and is often found on the "GL reports" menu. In QuickBooks, you will find it under the "file, print lists" menu, in Peachtree, look for "reports, general ledger, chart of accounts," and in One-Write Plus, it is available under "reports, financial."

General Ledger Listings

Trial Balance

As mentioned in the previous chapter, the trial balance is a listing of the ending balances in all of your accounts at a specific date. Although it is not mandatory to print this report every month, most businesses do it as a bird's-eye view of their financial situation and to prove that the accounts are in balance (debits = credits) before they print the many pages of the general ledger and financial statements. One important thing to look for in a trial balance is that the accounts look "normal" in magnitude. If your rent account goes from $1,800 after three months to $63,000 in the fourth month, you would be alerted that something went wrong.

In Figure 3-7 of the previous chapter, I presented a very simplified trial balance (take a look at it again); now in Figure 4-1, you can see the Peachtree sample company trial balance that is for a more complex business. This company maintains several categories of inventory, several categories of revenue, and separate accounts for every payroll deduction. You should consider which level of detail—the simplistic set of accounts of Figure 3-7 or the more complex version of Figure 4-1—better suits your business.

Figure 4-1: *Sample trial balance*

Bellweather Cleaning Services			
General Ledger Trial Balance			
As of Mar 31, 1995			
Account ID	**Account Description**	**Debit Amt**	**Credit Amt**
1000	Petty Cash	50.00	
1100	Cash in Savings	1,725.78	
1120	Cash in Checking	12,554.50	
1200	Accounts Receivable	8,715.65	
1205	Allowance for Bad Debt	150.00	
1300	Cleaning Supplies Inventory	1,525.17	
1310	Office Supplies Inventory	610.62	
1320	Product Inventory	1,438.65	

cont. on next page

Figure 4-1 cont.

Account ID	Account Description	Debit Amt	Credit Amt
1500	Prepaid Expenses	1,450.83	
1600	Furniture & Fixtures	8,801.28	
1710	Vehicles	21,330.00	
1720	Machinery & Equipment	2,545.25	
1799	Accumulated Depreciation		625.00
1800	Leasehold Improvements	20,000.00	
2000	Accounts Payable		2,811.15
2100	401K Deductions Payable		1,380.00
2130	Group Health Ins. Payable		1,456.21
2200	Notes Payable - Short Term		19,000.00
2300	Fed. Payroll W/H Tax - Payable		663.72
2310	State Payroll W/H Tax - Payable		258.94
2320	FICA Taxes - Payable		4,027.75
2330	FUTA Taxes - Payable		65.56
2340	SUTA Taxes - Payable		53.64
2350	Sales Tax Payable		1,213.72
2500	Notes Payable - First Nat.		17,350.00
2600	Capital Beginning of Year		36,456.85
2700	Owners Contribution	1,093.39	
3000	Commercial Services Revenues		8,135.00
3100	Residential Services Revenues		150.00
3200	Other Services Revenues		600.00
3225	Supplies Provided		2,154.48
3300	Interest Income		476.32
4000	Cost of Goods Sold	1,003.63	
5000	Salary Expenses Regular	7,662.50	
5005	Salary Overtime Expense	133.50	
5010	Employer Payroll Tax Expenses	892.68	
5100	Supplies Expense	578.65	
5200	Vehicle Expense	167.85	
5500	Bank Charges	25.00	
5600	Rent	675.00	
5830	Advertising/Marketing Expense	1,325.65	
5860	Contract Labor	1,665.00	
5900	Utilities Expense	757.76	
	Total:	96,878.34	96,878.34

General Ledger Detail

The trial balance shown in Figure 4-1 might be thought of as a summary general ledger listing, as it provides only the ending balance in each account. The detailed contents of each account over time is contained in the general ledger master file and should be printed periodically as the detailed general ledger listing. This is the basis for all your financial statements, so you would want to print its full contents at the end of each period (this could be monthly or quarterly—but at least annually).

Take a look at Figure 4-2, also from Peachtree. The general ledger detail would include the account ID, and/or account name, a beginning balance and, for each transaction, a date, a source journal (like PAY or CRJ), a description, a debit or credit amount, and an ending balance. *Note:* PAY means cash payments journal, CRJ means cash receipts journal, GENJ means general journal. The user specifies the date range that the report will cover. You can match the ending balances on the trial balance in Figure 4-1 to the ending balances on this detailed general ledger report of Figure 4-2. For example, Figure 4-1 lists a $1,725.78 balance in the "Cash in Savings" account and Figure 4-2 also shows this $1,725.78 balance in that account.

Figure 4-2: *Detailed general ledger audit trail*

Bellweather Cleaning Services
General Ledger
For the Period from Mar 1 to Mar 31

Account ID Account Descrip	Date	Reference	Trans Description	Jrnl	Debit Amt	Credit Amt	Balance
1000	3/1/95		Beginning Balance				50.00
Petty Cash	3/31/95		Current Change				
	3/31/95		Ending Balance				50.00
1100	3/1/95		Beginning Balance				1,500.00
Cash in Savings	3/1/95	BS-3/1		GEN	225.78		
	3/31/95		Current Change		225.78		225.78
	3/31/95		Ending Balance				1,725.78
1120	3/1/95		Beginning Balance				13,457.81
Cash in Checking	3/1/95	MAR 1	Hines Bicycle Repair	CRJ	815.50		
	3/1/95	3/1/95	CitiBank - Maine	CRJ	225.75		
	3/2/95	3/4/95	Corporate Computer Sale	CRJ	176.49		
	3/2/95	3/4/95	Cirus Office Leasing Gro	CRJ	358.70		
	3/2/95	5026	Mr. Sweeper Supplies	PAY		400.00	
	3/15/95	3/10/95	Cirus Office Leasing Gro	CRJ	566.70		
	3/15/95	1501	Davis Paper Supply	PAY		510.00	
	3/15/95	1502	Mr. Sweeper Supplies	PAY		380.00	
	3/15/95	2200	Steve Wayne Austin	PRJ		314.86	
	3/15/95	2201	Felicia Kessler	PRJ		330.06	
	3/15/95	2202	Kay J. Guillatt	PRJ		348.11	
	3/15/95	2203	Abbey Moore	PRJ		200.91	
	3/15/95	2204	Patti Rose Tremont	PRJ		252.51	
	3/23/95	5025	Sally's Catering Service	PAY		310.00	
	3/31/95		Current Change		2,143.14	3,046.45	-903.31
	3/31/95		Ending Balance				12,554.50

(this is a partial report)

After selecting the "detailed general ledger" for display, Peachtree will allow you to format and customize the listing by restricting it to a specific date range, a certain group of accounts (e.g., revenue only), specific columns to print on the listing, and it will allow you to collapse or expand the listing by showing sub-accounts separately or grouped. QuickBooks and One-Write Plus allow similar customizing choices.

Journal Reports

General Journal

You may have noticed in Figure 4-2, the detailed GL, that each transaction in an account shows a journal reference. A computer audit trail should clearly trace these entries to the original source of the transaction. It is common practice to print a cash receipts journal and sales journal (covered in Chapter 8), a cash payments journal and purchases journal (covered in Chapter 6), and any other journals that are posted to the GL. Some transactions are recorded in a general journal (discussed in the previous chapter), which is part of the GL module. It follows, then, that a listing of general journal entries should be printed at the end of each fiscal period. Figure 4-3 provides you with a sample general journal report from One-Write Plus.

Figure 4-3: *Sample general journal report*

TimsToo Services
GENERAL JOURNAL REPORT
1/1/96 TO 1/31/96

Date: 1/31/96   Ref No: Trans
Desc: Transfer cash from checking to savings

GL ACCOUNT NAME	DEBIT	CREDIT
1000 Checking Account	500.00	
1050 Savings Account		500.00
TOTAL:	500.00	500.00

Date: 1/31/96   Ref No: ADJ 1-1
Desc: Depreciation Expense

GL ACCOUNT NAME	DEBIT	CREDIT
6160 Depreciation Expense	88.00	
1571 A/D - Equipment		88.00
TOTAL:	88.00	88.00
GENERAL JOURNAL TOTAL:	588.00	588.00

Payroll Summary Journal

If you use the payroll module of an accounting package, all GL postings from payroll will be done automatically, and you will print various payroll reports from the payroll module (see Chapter 9). If your payroll is prepared by an out-side payroll service, you will receive a payroll summary report for each pay period. You will then make a general journal entry for the payroll summary and print that journal report in your accounting package to be sure it matches with the outside agency figures.

Financial Statements

Income Statements

Your income statement is a listing of all your revenue accounts, all your expense accounts, and the calculation of net income or loss (also called net profit or net earnings). An important accounting principle that governs the income state-ment is the "period" rule. An income statement is intended to report how the business progressed over a period of time. This statement will always carry a title that includes the prefix "for the period ending xxx." Let's start with a very simple example—here is the layout and format of an Income Statement:

Any Company
Income Statement
For the Month Ended 6/30/98

Sales revenue	$230,000
Cost of sales	- 170,000
Gross profit	60,000
Operating expenses	- 37,000
Net income	$23,000

Businesses that sell and/or manufacture a product need an expense category titled "cost of goods sold," followed by the calculation of "gross profit"—this represents the difference between the selling price and the cost of the goods you sell. The study of relationships between cost and sales price could, and often does, fill a whole textbook. We will touch on this a little further in a later chap-ter on inventory. Service businesses do not usually use these categories on their income statements.

It is common practice to produce income statements that report the current period (usually one month or one quarter) and an additional column for the year-to-date total for each line. The sample income statement from Peachtree in

Figure 4-4 shows the activity for the month of March, plus the activity for the current year to date.

Figure 4-4: *Sample income statement*

<table>
<tr><th colspan="5" align="center">**Bellweather Cleaning Services**
Income Statement
For the Three Months Ending March 31, 1995</th></tr>
<tr><td>**Revenues**</td><td>**March**</td><td>**% of Total Revenues**</td><td>**Year to Date**</td><td>**% of Total Revenue**</td></tr>
<tr><td>Commercial Services Revenues</td><td>$ 2,545.00</td><td>65.43</td><td>$ 6,905.00</td><td>69.18</td></tr>
<tr><td>Residential Services Revenues</td><td>100.00</td><td>2.57</td><td>150.00</td><td>1.50</td></tr>
<tr><td>Other Services Revenues</td><td>350.00</td><td>9.00</td><td>600.00</td><td>6.01</td></tr>
<tr><td>Supplies Provided</td><td>648.66</td><td>16.68</td><td>1,849.98</td><td>18.53</td></tr>
<tr><td>Interest Income</td><td><u>245.76</u></td><td>6.32</td><td><u>476.32</u></td><td>4.77</td></tr>
<tr><td>Total Revenues</td><td><u>3,889.42</u></td><td>100.00</td><td><u>9,981.30</u></td><td>100.00</td></tr>
<tr><td>Cost of Sales</td><td></td><td></td><td></td><td></td></tr>
<tr><td> Cost of Goods Sold</td><td><u>379.05</u></td><td>9.75</td><td><u>808.78</u></td><td>8.10</td></tr>
<tr><td>Total Cost of Sales</td><td><u>379.05</u></td><td>9.75</td><td><u>808.78</u></td><td>8.10</td></tr>
<tr><td>Gross Profit</td><td><u>3,510.37</u></td><td>90.25</td><td>9,172.52</td><td>91.90</td></tr>
<tr><td>Expenses</td><td></td><td></td><td></td><td></td></tr>
<tr><td> Salary Expenses Regular</td><td>1,747.50</td><td>44.93</td><td>7,662.50</td><td>76.77</td></tr>
<tr><td> Salary Overtime Expense</td><td>20.00</td><td>0.51</td><td>133.50</td><td>1.34</td></tr>
<tr><td> Employer Payroll Tax Expenses</td><td>202.39</td><td>5.20</td><td>892.68</td><td>8.94</td></tr>
<tr><td> Supplies Expense</td><td>94.89</td><td>2.44</td><td>555.47</td><td>5.57</td></tr>
<tr><td> Vehicle Expense</td><td>167.85</td><td>4.32</td><td>167.85</td><td>1.68</td></tr>
<tr><td> Bank Charges</td><td>25.00</td><td>0.64</td><td>25.00</td><td>0.25</td></tr>
<tr><td> Rent</td><td>225.00</td><td>5.78</td><td>675.00</td><td>6.76</td></tr>
<tr><td> Advertising/Marketing Expense</td><td>275.00</td><td>7.07</td><td>1,325.65</td><td>13.28</td></tr>
<tr><td> Contract Labor</td><td>0.00</td><td>0.00</td><td>2,430.00</td><td>24.35</td></tr>
<tr><td> Utilities Expense</td><td><u>198.95</u></td><td>5.12</td><td><u>757.76</u></td><td>7.59</td></tr>
<tr><td>Total Expenses</td><td><u>2,956.58</u></td><td>76.02</td><td><u>14,625.41</u></td><td>146.53</td></tr>
<tr><td>Net Income</td><td>$ <u>553.79</u></td><td>14.24</td><td>$ <u><5,452.88></u></td><td>54.63</td></tr>
</table>

There are many forms of the income statement. Some software will produce a single month statement, and some will automatically produce the type you see in Figure 4-4. Please notice that some percentage data is included—each item on the statement is expressed as a percentage of total revenue. For example, this sample statement tells us that advertising is 7.07 percent of revenue, and net income is 14.24 percent of revenue. The percentage of revenue column is extremely helpful when you are comparing your progress from month to month, and you can use these percentages when it comes time to prepare projected income statements. Peachtree and QuickBooks will also produce income statements that compare the current month of this year to the current month of last year *or* the current year-to-date statement to last year's year-to-date statement for the comparable period. If you are maintaining budget information, you will usually have the option of printing an income statement compared to budgeted amounts and the percentage variance from budget. All these reports are further customizable in Peachtree, QuickBooks, and One-Write Plus.

Another form of the income statement that is extremely helpful to business owners is one that lists multiple months side by side. Peachtree for Windows and One-Write Plus do not present revenue and expense for several months on one page, but QuickBooks does this easily. Figure 4-5 provides a glimpse of how helpful this can be for comparison purposes. QuickBooks can show many months (up to twelve side by side) and show percentages of revenue for each of those months.

Figure 4-5: *Comparative income statement*

Rock Castle Construction Profit and Loss July through September 1995				
	Jul '95	Aug '95	Sep '95	TOTAL
Ordinary Income/Expense				
Income				
Construction	54,160	39,830	38,863	133,303
Total Income	54,610	39,830	38,863	133,303
Cost of Goods Sold				
Cost of Goods Sold	124	890	699	1,712
Total COGS	124	890	699	1,712
Gross Profit	54,486	38,941	38,164	131,591
Expense				
Telephone	45	45	44	133
Automobile Expense	49	65	46	160
Freight & Delivery	60	0	0	60
Insurance	739	372	0	1,111
Interest Expense	322	319	381	1,022
Job Expenses	41,730	7,150	19,430	68,310
Payroll Expenses	7,234	7,923	7,379	22,537
Rent	900	900	900	2,700
Utilities	81	95	85	261
Total Expense	51,160	16,869	28,265	96,294
Net Ordinary Income	3,326	22,071	9,899	35,297
Net Income	**3,326**	**22,071**	**9,899**	**35,297**

Balance Sheets

The balance sheet is a statement of the company's financial condition at a specific point in time. It contains a list of the company's assets, its liabilities, and its owner equity (see definitions in Chapter 3). The GAAP that governs the balance sheet is the principle of the continuing equality of components in the basic accounting equation: Assets = Liabilities + Owner Equity. A quick glimpse at a balance sheet shows that ending balances from the GL are arranged this way:

Any Company
Balance Sheet
6/30/98

ASSETS:	
Cash	$2,500
Accounts receivable	$7,890
Inventory	$12,300
Total assets	$22,690
LIABILITIES:	
Accounts payable	$5,690
Notes payable	$6,500
Total liabilities	$12,190
OWNER EQUITY:	
Jean Jones, Capital	$7,000
Retained earnings	$3,500
Total liabilities and capital	$22,690

It is very important for you to understand the difference between the balance sheet and the income statement. Remember, the income statement contains a view of how you've done over a period of time. The balance sheet, on the other hand, is a snapshot on a specific date. For example, the cash balance you see on the balance sheet is the cash amount on hand for the date of the statement, but cash will undoubtedly change tomorrow and most days this week.

Figure 4-6 provides an example of a balance sheet from One-Write Plus. This financial statement can get quite sophisticated when it shows more than one date and contains many subcategories. The most common categories are current assets, long-term assets, current liabilities, long-term liabilities, and owner capital. "Current" refers to assets or obligations that will turn over in less than a year; "long-term" refers to assets or debts that will remain on your records for more than a year. You can see that your inventory is a current asset, but plant assets (like equipment) are long-term assets. It is important to note that the total dollar amount of the assets is, of course, equal to the total of the liabilities plus owner equity.

As noted in the previous chapter, "equity" is a concept that refers to the owner's interest in the business. The amount of the original investment is usually recorded in an account called "capital" or "capital stock" or "paid in

Figure 4-6: *Sample balance sheet*

TimsToo Services		
BALANCE SHEET		
January 31, 1996		
ASSETS		
CURRENT ASSETS		
Checking Account	$ 4,021.79	
Savings Account	2,000.00	
Undeposited Cash	2,000.00	
Accounts Receivable	1,483.45	
TOTAL CURRENT ASSETS		$ 9,505.24
PROPERTY AND EQUIPMENT		
Equipment	$ 5,700.00	
A/D - Equipment	(510.00)	
Furniture and Fixtures	2,560.00	
A/D - Furniture & Fixtures	(187.00)	
Vehicles	12,700.00	
A/D Vehicles	(1,325.00)	
TOTAL PROPERTY AND EQUIPMENT		$18,938.00
TOTAL ASSETS		$28,443.24
LIABILITIES AND EQUITY		
CURRENT LIABILITIES		
Accounts Payable	$ 122.50	
Credit Card - Visa	1,856.65	
Notes Payable - Short Term	10,800.00	
Employee Health Ins Payable	56.31	
401K Payable	45.90	
Sales Taxes Payable	74.80	
Payroll Taxes Payable	281.33	
Accrued Taxes	402.55	
TOTAL CURRENT LIABILITIES		$13,640.04

cont. on next page

Figure 4–6 cont.

TOTAL CURRENT LIABILITIES			$13,640.04
EQUITY			
Common Stock	$	13,500.00	
Retained Earnings		658.60	
Net Income (Loss)		644.60	
TOTAL EQUITY			$14,803.20
TOTAL LIABILITIES AND EQUITY			$28,443.24

capital." As net income is earned by a business, the owner's investment grows; when withdrawals are made by the owner (or dividends paid to stockholders), the investment declines. If you see a negative amount of retained earnings on a balance sheet, you can assume that the company is accumulating net losses. The point to be understood here is that the net income of the business should be reflected on the balance sheet as a positive amount in the owner equity section. In Figure 4-6, you see this "income" as a positive amount because this company had a net income in January. "Retained earnings" is the accumulated net income from previous periods.

Cash Flow Statements

Have you heard this common small business query: "Where did all the cash go?" A business usually wants to know what its cash position is and how the company got to that position. Therefore, the statement of cash flow has become a standard item in the financial statement package. An example of this statement from Peachtree for Windows is shown in Figure 4-7. Unfortunately, QuickBooks and One-Write Plus do not provide a statement of cash flow.

Figure 4-7: *Sample statement of cash flows*

Bellweather Cleaning Services		
Statement of Cash Flow		
For the Three Months Ended March 31,1995		
	Current Month	**Year to Date**
Cash Flows from operating activities		
Net Income	$ <190.54>	$ <7,832.81>
Adjustments to reconcile net		
income to net cash provided		
by operating activities		
Accumulated Depreciation	$ 128.00	$ 128.00
Accounts Receivable	$ <3,783.40>	$ <2,680.90>
Cleaning Supplies Inventory	478.93	80.69
Product Inventory	1,437.73	900.71
Accounts Payable	$ 2,477.80	<2,076.75>
Salaries Payable	200.00	200.00
401 K Deductions Payable	25.00	180.00
Notes Payable - Short Term	<265.50>	<265.50>
FICA Taxes - Payable	563.08	3,062.65
Sales Tax Payable	199.84	470.44
Total Adjustments	1,461.48	<0.66>
Net Cash Provided by Operations	1,270.94	<7,833.47>
Cash Flows from investing activities		
Used for		
Vehicles	$ <2,400.00>	$ <2,400.00>
Leasehold Improvements	<850.00>	<850.00>
Net cash used in investing	<3,250.00>	<3,250.00>
Cash Flows from financing activities		
Proceeds From		
Owner's Contributions	$ 850.00	$ 850.00
Used For	———	———
Net cash used in financing	850.00	850.00
Net increase <decrease> in cash	$ <1,129.06>	$ <10,233.47>
Summary		
Cash Balance at End of Period	$ 13,878.75	$ 13,878.75
Cash Balance at Beginning of Period	$ <15,007.81>	$ <24,112.22>
Net Increase <Decrease> in Cash	$ <1,129.06>	$ <10,233.47>

At the most basic level, a statement of cash flow shows the cash inflows and out-flows resulting from various business activities. For purposes of clarity, the cash inflows and outflows are broken down into three categories: the cash activity resulting from operations (that is the day-to-day business of earning revenue and paying expenses); the cash flow resulting from investment activities (like the purchase and sale of plant assets); and those cash activities resulting from financing activities (those transactions involving loans, new infusions of capital, or payouts of dividends). These cash details are followed by a summary listing ending cash, beginning cash, and the net increase (or decrease) in cash.

Important Note: A cash budget differs from a cash flow statement in that the for-mer is a plan for the future (a cash forecast), while the latter documents the recent history of cash flow activities. There is no low-end accounting package that prepares cash budgets, although QuickBooks and One-Write Plus do offer a limited cash forecast for a restricted future period.

Study Figure 4-7 for a moment, and you will see that both income statement data and balance sheet data are used in the statement of cash flow. The beginning bal-ance in an account of one period is subtracted from the ending balance of that period in order to determine how much cash flowed through. Take, for example, the notes payable–short term line; the amount there was determined when the software took the beginning period balance in this account (found on the bal-ance sheet) and subtracted the ending period balance (from the balance sheet) to create this statement of cash flow. If this account decreases, then cash must have been used to pay off part of the loan. The computer does all this for you, and after a few months of studying your own cash flow statement, you will under-stand better how the statement is constructed and how you can best use it.

Graphs for Management Analysis

Peachtree for Windows provides graphic reports in the receivables, payables, and inventory module but does not offer graphs of the general ledger summary data, and One-Write Plus offers no graphs at all. QuickBooks does the best job of presenting graphs of the financial statement data. Figure 4-8 provides you with a sample from this package. The bar graph in this figure provides you with a pictorial view of the revenue and expenses for a seven-month period. With this type of presentation, you can instantly see that the best revenue months are June and July, with the largest net profit gained in August. The expense pie chart clearly shows that "job expenses" and "payroll" are the two biggest expenses and that job expenses comprised more than three-quarters of the total expenses during this period. Once you print these graphs for a few periods and compare them, you can easily see trends that help you to predict income and expenses.

Figure 4-8: *Revenue and expense graph from QuickBooks*

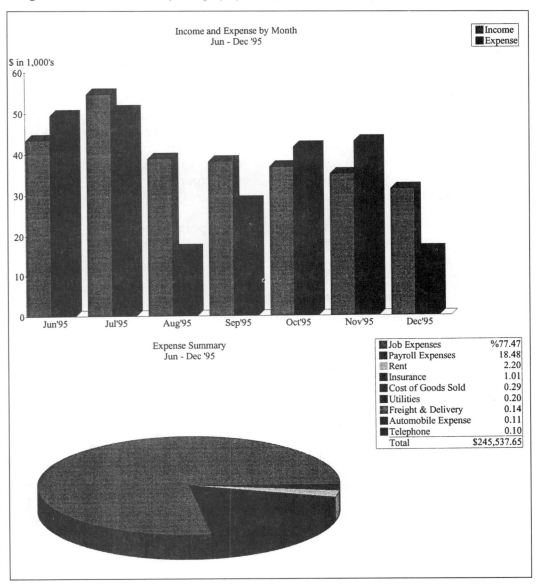

You can create unlimited graphs from any accounting data once you export your financial statement data to a spreadsheet program. Get started on this path by reading the "Exporting General Ledger Reports to Other Software" section later in this chapter, as well as the "exporting" topics in Chapters 6 and 8.

What to Save/What to Ignore

Your general ledger software has the capability to produce more reports than you will ever need. When you first start working with a GL system, it is a good idea to experiment with all the various reports each module provides. You will need to match the information provided on the reports with your needs and personal preferences. Try to keep in mind that your business history is represented by your accounting reports, and choose among the available reports that allow you to make comparisons. In other words, print reports on a periodic basis that can be compared to previous periods for growth and general business health. You will find right away that it is helpful to compare each period's income statement to the previous few periods. Experience will tell you how often you need to review this data.

My recommendation for the minimum set of GL reports to be printed and filed for each period in a book or folder is:

- the general journal listing
- the general ledger detail report
- the income statement (you choose the best style)
- the balance sheet
- the statement of cash flow (when available)

While not part of your accounting records, you will also want to file whatever graphs you found useful.

Year-End Closing Procedures

This section will give a very brief explanation of the concept of year-end closing, but I strongly recommend that you seek advice from your accountant before taking this step. At the end of a fiscal year (a date determined by you or your accountant, not necessarily December 31), there is an accounting procedure that is required by accounting principles called "closing the books." What this means is that the revenue and expense accounts are summarized and closed to the owners capital or retained earnings account. This means that net income is added to owner equity, or net loss is deducted from owner equity. Remember that the revenue and expense accounts are just subcategories of owner equity. These accounts "collect" revenue and expense over the year, but in order to start each new fiscal year with a clean slate, these accounts are closed to owner equity. All you have to do is tell your accounting software to perform the procedure—the computer does the rest.

Peachtree will notify you if any transactions have not been posted to accounts and then post them for you, and the program will not continue unless you print (to paper) all the journals and a yearly general ledger detail report. QuickBooks and One-Write Plus display a warning that this closes some accounts and suggests you make a backup copy of all files before proceeding. But once those tasks are done, the program resets the revenue and expense accounts to zero.

Once you complete the closing procedure, you should print a trial balance dated the first day of your new accounting year. Figure 4-9, from Peachtree, provides an example of this new beginning trial balance (the old-fashioned name for this report is the post-closing trial balance). The important point to note is that only the assets, liabilities, and owner equity accounts retain their balances at this point. All other accounts have been closed, and their balances have been transferred into a retained earnings or owner's capital account; in other words, the revenue and expense accounts have zero balances.

Figure 4-9: *Consequences of closing the accounts*

<table>
<tr><td colspan="4" align="center">**Bellweather Cleaning Services**
General Ledger Trial Balance
January 1, 1995</td></tr>
<tr><td>**Account ID**</td><td>**Account Description**</td><td>**Debit Amt**</td><td>**Credit Amt**</td></tr>
<tr><td>1000</td><td>Petty Cash</td><td>50.00</td><td></td></tr>
<tr><td>1100</td><td>Cash in Savings</td><td>1,500.00</td><td></td></tr>
<tr><td>1120</td><td>Cash in Checking</td><td>16,715.60</td><td></td></tr>
<tr><td>1200</td><td>Accounts Receivable</td><td>4852.23</td><td></td></tr>
<tr><td>1300</td><td>Cleaning Supplies Inventory</td><td>1,001.25</td><td></td></tr>
<tr><td>1320</td><td>Product Inventory</td><td>1,781.93</td><td></td></tr>
<tr><td>1710</td><td>Vehicles</td><td>20,000.00</td><td></td></tr>
<tr><td>1799</td><td>Accumulated Depreciation</td><td></td><td>125.00</td></tr>
<tr><td>1800</td><td>Leasehold Improvements</td><td>20,000.00</td><td></td></tr>
<tr><td>2000</td><td>Accounts Payable</td><td></td><td>2,837.70</td></tr>
<tr><td>2100</td><td>401 K Deductions Payable</td><td></td><td>1,200.00</td></tr>
<tr><td>2130</td><td>Group Health Ins. Payable</td><td></td><td>1,456.21</td></tr>
<tr><td>2200</td><td>Notes Payable - Short Term</td><td></td><td>19,000.00</td></tr>
<tr><td>2300</td><td>Fed. Payroll W/H Tax - Payable</td><td></td><td>63.72</td></tr>
<tr><td>2310</td><td>State Payroll W/H Tax - Payable</td><td></td><td>18.94</td></tr>
<tr><td>2320</td><td>FICA Taxes - Payable</td><td></td><td>1,798.34</td></tr>
<tr><td>2330</td><td>FUTA Taxes - Payable</td><td></td><td>15.56</td></tr>
<tr><td>2340</td><td>SUTA Taxes - Payable</td><td></td><td>13.64</td></tr>
<tr><td>2350</td><td>Sales Tax Payable</td><td></td><td>368.36</td></tr>
<tr><td>2500</td><td>Notes Payable - First Nat.</td><td></td><td>19,350.00</td></tr>
<tr><td>2600</td><td>Capital - Beginning of Year</td><td></td><td>19,653.54</td></tr>
</table>

cont. on next page

Figure 4–9 cont.

Account ID	Account Description	Debit Amt	Credit Amt
2700	Owner's Contributions		
3000	Commercial Services Revenues		
3100	Residential Services Revenues		
3200	Other Services Revenues		
3225	Supplies Provided		
3300	Interest Income		
3350	Shipping Charges Reimbursed		
399	Misc Income		
4000	Cost of Goods Sold		
4500	Cost of Sale Shipping/Handling		
5000	Salary Expenses Regular		
5005	Salary Overtime Expense		
5010	Employer Payroll Taxes Expenses		
5100	Supplies Expense		
5200	Vehicle Expense		
5500	Bank Charges		
5550	Interest Expense		
5600	Rent		
5700	General Liab. Insurance Exp.		
5710	Vehicle Insurance Expense		
5720	Fire & Theft Insurance Expense		
5730	Group Health Insurance Expense		
5810	Postage Expense		
5820	Accounting & Legal Expense		
5830	Advertising/Marketing Expense		
5835	Entertainment and Travel		
5860	Contract Labor		
5900	Utilities Expense		
5999	Miscellaneous Expenses		
6000	Depreciation Expense		
	Total:	65,901.01	65,901.01

Exporting General Ledger Reports to Other Software

We have already discovered a situation where we might want financial statement data to be placed in our spreadsheet software—so that we can produce graphs. One company likes to have its cost of sales in each revenue category placed side by side, with the revenue in that same category, and with the gross profit placed in the third column. These examples are good reasons for exporting accounting data to a spreadsheet. In addition, there may be times when you want to use a portion of your accounting data in a word processing document. Figure 4-10 provides an example of a Quattro Pro spreadsheet with financial statement data compressed into a short form for internal use. Here's a general introduction to the steps you must follow to produce this.

Figure 4-10: *Quattro Pro spreadsheet using general ledger data*

	A	B	C	D	E
1	Revenue and Expense Summary at March 31, 1998				
2	From Peachtree, Bellweather Cleaning Services				
3					
4	Account ID	Account Description	Net-Period End 3/31/95		
5					
6	3000	Commercial Services Revenues		$3,650.00	
7	3100	Residential Services Revenues		$100.00	
8	3200	Other Services Revenues		$450.00	
9	3225	Supplies Sales Revenue		$947.86	
10	3250	Discounts Allowed		($22.50)	
11	3300	Interest Income		$245.76	
12	4000	Cost of Goods Sold	$584.05		
13	5000	Salary Expenses Regular	$2,317.50		
14	5005	Salary Overtime Expense	$68.00		
15	5010	Employer Payroll Tax Expe	$270.22		
16	5100	Supplies Expense	$358.34		
17	5150	Discounts Taken	($10.50)		
18	5200	Vehicle Expense	$167.85		
19	5500	Bank Charges	$25.00		
20	5600	Rent	$225.00		
21	5830	Advertising/Marketing Expe	$275.00		
22	5900	Utilities Expense	$198.95		
23					
24		Total Revenue		$5,371.12	
25		Total Expense	$4,479.41		
26		Net Income		$891.71	
27					
28					

The process for exporting data from Peachtree for Windows to another application software package generally involves these steps (QuickBooks and One-Write Plus follow similar procedures):

1. Display and/or print the report in the GL that most closely resembles the data you want in your spreadsheet or word processor.

2. Select the "file" and "export" commands from the menu.

3. Determine which fields to export and what type of export file to create (e.g., a text file, a tab delimited data file, or a brand of spreadsheet file) and where to store it (e.g., the A: drive, or C:\xxx).

4. Open your spreadsheet or word processor software and use the "file, import," "tools, import," "file, open," or "file, retrieve" command to open the file saved in the third step.

At this point, the list of items from your GL file can be manipulated within the spreadsheet or word processing document. Reference to your user's manuals for both the accounting package and the word processing or spreadsheet package is usually necessary to gain competence with importing and exporting files. The best approach is to try it out and see what results. Call the technical support line at your software vendor for specific guidance.

Chapter Five

Purchases and Accounts Payable

Introduction to the Purchasing and Accounts Payable Functions

The use of an accounts payable (AP) system allows you to manage purchases, track vendor accounts, pay your bills on time, write checks, and even reconcile your checking account. You can enter your repetitive payments (rent, electric bill, mortgage payment, etc.) just once and "recall" them each month when you need them. With accounting software, you are assured of accurate expense recording for tax time, as well as controls that assure you of timely and useful operating reports for purchasing and payment activity. In other words, an accounts payable system is not just for tracking "payables"—it is the key to all payments your business must make, even if they do not involve the use of credit.

In accounting terms, when a purchase is made on credit (whether it be a purchase of services or a purchase of tangible goods), an expense or asset account should be increased, while the accounts payable account is also increased. When payment is actually made for this account, the accounts payable account is decreased and the cash account is decreased. When a purchase is made for cash (that is, a check is written immediately), the accounting functions are simpler. At the time of purchase, an expense or asset account is increased, and the cash account is decreased.

This chapter explains the procedures used to record the purchases and payments commonly made by small businesses. The goal here is to help you understand how

Note: The accrual method of accounting is assumed in the discussions in this chapter. See Chapter 3 for an explanation of accrual basis accounting.

the data is entered and what the computer does with this data. The many reports produced by an accounts payable system are detailed in the following chapter.

Bird's-Eye View of an Accounts Payable System

The "navigation aid" from the Peachtree for Windows display provides a nut-shell view of how accounts payable components work.

Figure 5-1: *Navigation aid for accounts payable from Peachtree*

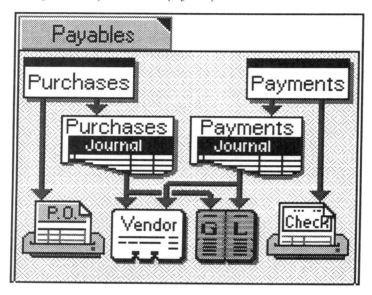

From this illustration, you can see that purchases and payments are the two major inputs to a payables system. These transactions are recorded on purchase invoices and check forms, then collected into the purchases journal and the payments journal (sometimes called the cash disbursements journal.) The purchase and payment transactions are then copied to a vendor ledger and the appropriate general ledger accounts by the computer. These are the main components of an AP system that are to be discussed in detail in this chapter.

The Inner Workings of an Accounts Payable System

A more detailed flowchart of AP elements and procedures is shown in Figure 5-2. Let's study this figure very closely in order to understand the documents used, the input data required, and the outputs produced.

Figure 5-2: *Accounts Payable (AP) data flow*

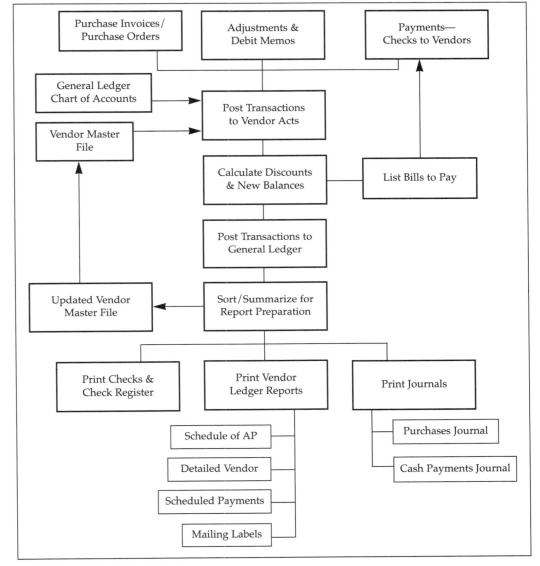

Input

The most common input files and documents for the AP system are:

- the vendor master file (sometimes called the vendor ledger)
- the general ledger (GL) chart of accounts file
- the purchase invoice data

- the payment data
- any adjustments (debit memos)

The vendor master file and the GL chart of accounts are the reference files for the preparation of purchase invoices and checks. These files contain the permanent information about vendors and account categories (covered in Chapter 3). Some accounting packages, like Peachtree for Windows, allow you to enter data that produces the actual purchase order, while other systems that do not actually print purchase orders require you to enter purchase data on a screen titled "enter bills" from whatever invoices you receive from your vendors. If goods are returned or adjustments on the bill are granted (called debit memos), these are corrections that also must be entered in the AP records.

Processing

The basic processing that occurs within an AP system includes:

- the posting of purchases and payments to individual vendor accounts
- the calculation of discounts, due dates, and new balances for vendors
- the display of scheduled bills to pay
- the summarization and posting of amounts to appropriate GL accounts

This last step assumes the "integration" of AP with the general ledger files. This means that AP transactions are automatically posted to GL accounts (see Chapter 3 for an explanation of GL and posting). The computer, of course, is legendary for fast calculation of due dates, discounts, invoice totals, and new account balances. Your AP system will also be able to present you with a list of all unpaid bills up to a specified date so that you can pick the ones you want to pay from that list. After this processing is complete, the computer organizes the AP files for the production of any other reports you may want from your purchases and accounts payable records.

Output

The most common outputs from an AP system are:

- the transaction journals (purchases journal and cash payments journal)
- the checks to be sent to vendors
- various vendor ledger balance listings

The journals normally produced are the purchases journals and cash disbursements journal (or payments journal). These journals show how the purchases and payments have been posted to the general ledger. For example, transactions will cause increases in accounts ranging from supplies and prepaid insurance to legal expenses to postage expense. Debit memos and internal adjustments will be reported as negative transactions in the purchases journal. An obviously important reason for utilizing an AP system is to be able to write checks quickly and accurately.

The vendor ledger balance listings are various presentations of the detailed information that is held in the AP ledger—that is, you should be able to see the list of ending balances for all vendors, or just the recent history on one vendor, or the detailed transactions for a specified period of time for all vendors. Some AP packages also provide for a mailing label printout. More sophisticated AP systems might also provide for a cleared and outstanding check listing used in bank reconciliations. These reports are detailed further in Chapter 6.

The Vendor Master File

Remember that a master file is the basic set of information about vendors, customers, or employees that is used repeatedly in the processing of transactions. The chart of accounts master file was introduced in Chapter 3. The vendor master file contains names and addresses and other unchanging information about each vendor. A vendor is any individual or business that goods or services are purchased from and that will be named as a payee when writing checks. The following are some of the items normally found in a vendor master file:

- vendor ID code (both alpha and numeric)
- vendor name
- vendor address, phone, and fax numbers
- contact person's name
- discount and payment terms
- vendor type (e.g., supplies, inventory, contractor, etc.)
- default general ledger purchase account numbers
- purchase history for that vendor
- current balance owed

An example record within a vendor master file from Peachtree for Windows is shown in Figure 5-3. The "purchase default" accounts and "history" are found on the cards behind the "general" card that is shown in the figure.

Figure 5-3: *Sample vendor master file record*

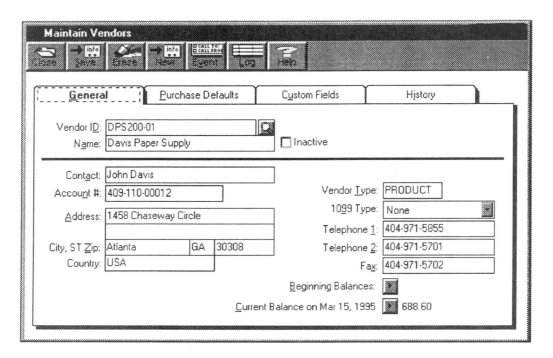

The vendor master file plays a central role in AP processing because every purchase or payment transaction will require that a vendor name or number be entered. The user can access a table of vendors that are already contained in the vendor master file and select one for the current transaction. Most AP systems allow you to type the first few letters of a vendor name, and as soon as the computer recognizes the vendor, it will provide the rest of the name and any pertinent items from the master file. For example, in Figure 5-3 we only typed "davi" before the computer recognized this vendor as "Davis Paper Supply" and displayed all the stored data for this vendor.

If the vendor being served is not already in the master file, the AP package will notify the user that the vendor does not exist and will encourage the user to enter all necessary data to create a new record in the master file. This is called creating new master records "on-the-fly." Figure 5-3 actually is an example of the Peachtree screen that pops up when creating a new vendor record or updating an existing record.

Links with the Chart of Accounts

Purchase and payment transactions also rely heavily on the complete list of accounts in the general ledger—called the chart of accounts and described in detail in Chapter 3. Think of it, whenever a purchase is made, an increase in an asset or expense account is required. This could be office supplies, furniture, automobiles, machinery, prepaid insurance, rent expense, legal expense, utilities expense, entertainment expense, postage expense, etc. Some purchase transactions require an increase in multiple asset or expense accounts. The important point here is that the GL chart of accounts will probably need to be viewed, and an item selected, for each purchase or payment transaction.

Small business accounting software makes this easy by displaying a default GL account for each purchase transaction that was specified when you set up the vendor record. In Figure 5-3, the GL Purchase account is named on the "purchase defaults" tab. During AP data entry, this GL purchase account becomes the default account. You can always look at a pop-up chart of accounts and select another account if you wish. See Figure 5-4 for an example from One-Write Plus. The background of the illustration displays a part of the purchases entry screen that will be described in detail in the next section; when the cursor is in the "account no." field, a mouse-click rolls down the chart of accounts list seen in the bottom half of the illustration. You simply double-click the account you want to charge for this purchase, and you are on your way to quick completion of the purchase transaction.

Figure 5-4: *Sample chart of accounts selection*

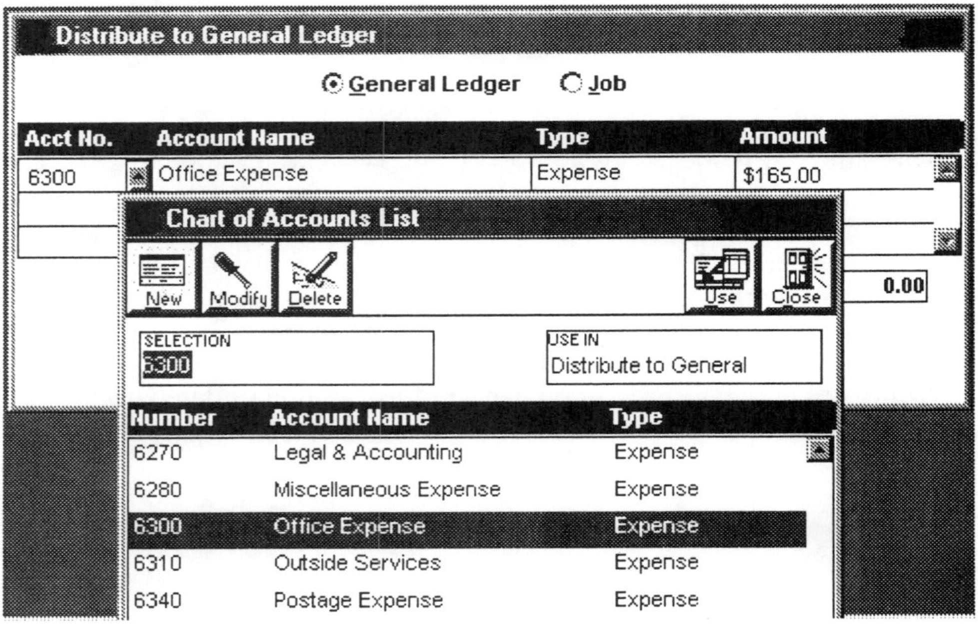

Entering Purchase Invoices

The Accounting behind Purchases on Account

The purchase of goods or services is just the first step in business operations that eventually leads to inventory management, cash management, expense analysis, and the determination of net profit. The purchase of goods or services on account causes an increase in business assets or expenses and causes an increase in accounts payable. In accounting terms, this means recording the transaction as a debit to the asset (e.g., furniture) or expense (e.g., postage expense) and a credit to accounts payable. When a purchase transaction is entered into your computerized accounting system, the transaction will be automatically debited to the accounts you name and automatically credited to accounts payable, as well as being recorded in a vendor record. For example, a bill for legal services would be recorded as a debit to legal expense and a credit to accounts payable

Purchase Data Entry

The data for a purchase on account is normally entered on a data entry screen titled "purchases" or "enter bills." A sample of this screen from QuickBooks is shown in Figure 5-5. Please notice that, at the bottom of the screen, there is a tab (like the tab on a file folder) for purchases of "items" and another tab for the purchases of "expenses." The "items" tab is for inventory items, and the "expenses" tab is for goods or services that are not inventory items. I will explain the purchase of inventory items first.

Once the user enters a vendor name, the vendor address and terms of sale are automatically filled in from the vendor master file. The current date is given as a default date, but the user can over-type any appropriate date. The reference number field is blank so you can enter the vendor's invoice number (usually optional). If the user enters a quantity and item name on the "items" tab of this screen, the computer fills in the description, unit price, and total price for that item (if it is in the master file). In the example, the user entered under "Qty" (quantity) 8 and selected "hardware: locks" from an inventory list; the description, unit cost, and amount were brought in from the master files. Multiple items on one invoice are entered in the same way, and the total is updated accordingly. The transaction in this illustration will be debited (charged) to the inventory account and credited (increased) to accounts payable.

Figure 5-5: *Purchase transaction entry*

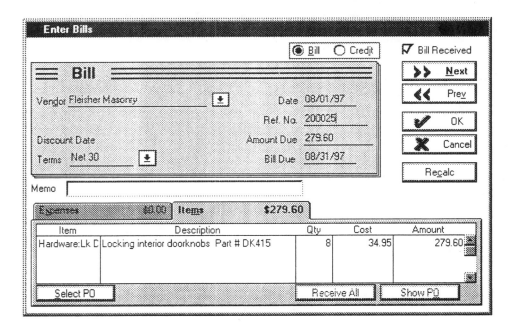

If you activate the "expenses" tab of the screen in Figure 5-5, you can click on the "account" field to view a pop-up chart of accounts and select the appropriate account for this purchase. This process was described in the previous section.

The "due date" and "discount date" in the lower section of the "bill" are automatically calculated by QuickBooks, based on the payment "terms" existing for this vendor on the vendor master file record. The "purchase defaults" tab of Figure 5-3 contains a section that specifies terms such as "2% 10, Net 30." This means that we can take a 2 percent discount if we pay within ten days or pay the net amount in thirty days. Since the invoice in Figure 5-5 was dated April 20, we can take a discount if we pay by April 30, but the final due date is May 20 with no discount. The software calculates these dates and the discount amount for us!

Posting Purchase Transactions

Once a purchase transaction screen is complete, it should be saved and posted (copied) to the appropriate accounts. Most accounting packages will include a "post" command within its menus or icons. You can see several illustrations in this book where Peachtree offers an icon (or command) to "post" the transaction. One-Write Plus uses an icon labeled "save," while QuickBooks simply wants you to click on "OK" (look on the right edge of Figure 5-5). When this command (post, save, or OK) is executed, the computer will save the transaction and post (copy) it to the accounts payable GL account, to the vendor account, and to the appropriate general ledger expense or asset accounts (described earlier in this section).

A listing of purchase transactions is normally displayed or printed by producing a purchases journal. You may be able to more completely understand the posting process for the purchase invoice by looking at a sample of the purchases journal and a general ledger account. Figure 5-6 shows a transaction for the purchase of promotional flyers on account in a purchases journal from Peachtree. The bottom half of Figure 5-6 shows how the debit from the transaction would appear in the general ledger account, #5830, Advertising/Marketing Expense, after posting. As you can see, one line of the journal is copied (posted) to one account in the general ledger. A similar process occurs for every transaction in an accounting system.

Figure 5-6: *Purchases journal posted to general ledger*

Bellweather Cleaning Services
Purchase Journal

Date	Account ID Account Description	Invoice #	Line Description	Debit Amt	Credit Amt
3/9/95	5830 Advertising/Marketing Expense 2000 Accounts Payable	6091-99	Flyers for March Promo; black & white; 5000 units Speedy Printer Service	275.00	275.00

Bellweather Cleaning Services
General Ledger

Account ID Account Description	Date Reference	Jrnl	Trans Description	Debit Amt	Credit Amt	Balance
5830 Advertising/Marketing Expense	3/1/95		Beginning Balance			1,050.65
	3/9/95 6091-99	PJ	Speedy Printer Service– Flyers for March Promo; black & white; 5000 units	275.00		
			Current Period Change	275.00		275.00
	3/31/95		**Ending Balance**			**1,325.65**

Choosing Items for Payment

Payments on Account

Purchase transactions that have been entered into an AP system can be paid immediately (for example, the purchase of stamps at the local USPS), or can be scheduled for payment at a later date. If a transaction was entered on the "purchases" or "enter bills" data entry screen presented in the previous section, the purchase invoice will be available for selection on the payment transaction screen when it is time to write the check for that transaction. For example, we entered a purchase transaction in QuickBooks from Fleischer Masonry on April 20, with a due date of May 20; this purchase will appear on the payment screen for Fleischer Masonry until you have paid it. Figure 5-7 provides an example of the data entry screen for a payment in the Peachtree for Windows software.

Figure 5-7: *Payment transaction entry*

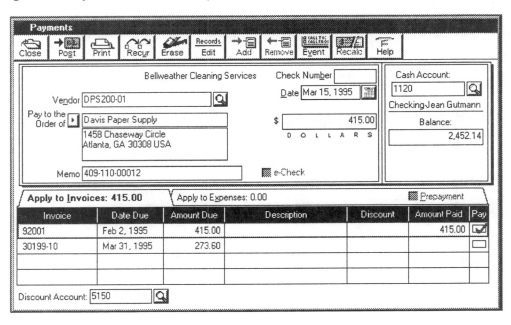

Once a vendor name is entered on this screen, the vendor name and address, current date, and the currently unpaid invoices for that vendor are brought up automatically. Notice at the bottom of Figure 5-7 that there is a tab (like the tab at the top of a file folder) labeled "apply to invoices." When you click on this tab, all unpaid purchase invoices for the selected vendor will appear on this open folder. To pay one of these unpaid invoices, you simply need to click in the "pay" column at the bottom of the screen next to each invoice you wish to pay. If a discount is appropriate (based on the date of the check and the original date of the invoice), it will show in the "discount" field. If you want to make a partial payment, you would enter an "amount paid" for that invoice. Once the payment amounts are entered at the bottom of this screen, the check amount is automatically calculated and displayed in the "dollars" field. When you specify "post" for this transaction, the computer will automatically debit (decrease) both the accounts payable and vendor account, and will credit (decrease) the cash account.

Selecting Payment Items from a List

An alternative to the above procedure would be to view all vendors who are waiting to be paid and then to mark the ones you want to pay. Peachtree has a "select for payment" option on its "tasks" menu, and QuickBooks and One-Write Plus have a "pay bills" option. This alternative presents you with a list of all previously entered purchase invoices for all vendors that have not yet been paid (see Figure 5-8 for an example from One-Write Plus). The user simply checks off the items to pay (notice the "pay" column in Figure 5-8) and the total to be paid at the bottom of the screen. If there are several payments to one vendor, they will be combined on one check.

Figure 5-8: *Selecting payments from a list*

Vendor Name	Ref No	Due Dt	Disc Dt	Disc Amt	Invoice Bal	Pay	Disc Taken	Amount Paid
A - Z Supply	00098243	3/9/96	2/18/96	$15.05	$673.89	☐	$0.00	$0.00
Creative Advertising	00006374	3/20/96	2/29/96	$18.55	$927.34	☒	$18.55	$908.79
Strings & Things	00000835	3/20/96	2/29/96	$1.66	$83.13	☒	$1.66	$81.47

Pay Bills — Apply — Report — Cancel

VENDORS: All Vendors
CATEGORY: All Categories
BANK ACCOUNT: Checking Account
CHECK DATE: 2/29/96
CUTOFF DATE: 2/29/96
Beginning Bank Balance: $6,987.14

Totals: $20.21 $990.26
Ending Bank Balance: $5,996.88

Requesting Checks without Previously Entered Bills

Did you notice that there is another tab near the bottom of Figure 5-7 labeled "apply to expenses?" If you click on this tab, you may enter a payment to a vendor that was not previously scheduled on account. That is, you can specify the account number to be charged for a check that will be written immediately, like buying those postage stamps. This type of transaction will result in a debit (increase) to the expense account you specify and a credit (decrease) to the cash account when posted to the general ledger accounts. This transaction would not affect a vendor account in the accounts payable ledger.

Producing Checks

When the payments described in the previous section are posted, the accounting work on them is complete, but, of course, you will still want to produce the physical checks to mail to the vendors. In Figure 5-7, you may have noticed the "check" icon—with paper protruding from a printer. In Peachtree, you click this check icon after each payment transaction you enter in order to print a check at that time, or you can postpone all check printing until a later time. If you choose to do the latter, you can select "reports, accounts payable, checks" from the menu, and then specify dates and beginning check number in order to print any unprinted checks. A sample check, with payment information stub, is shown in Figure 6-1 at the beginning of the next chapter. Printing a check register would then be appropriate—this will also be covered in the next chapter.

Recurring (Memorized) Transactions

Every business experiences repetitive transactions that normally occur every month or quarter. Some examples are your insurance premium payments, your rent payments, mortgage payments, and other loan payments. In these cases, you know that a check for the rent must be written on the first of every month, or the mortgage payment requires a check on the fifteenth of each month. In QuickBooks and One-Write Plus, these are known as memorized transactions; Peachtree calls them recurring transactions.

In QuickBooks, after entering data for a purchase invoice or payment transaction that recurs on a regular basis, you would select "edit, memorize" from the menu to save a copy of the transaction for future use. A dialog box will appear that asks you to specify how often the transaction recurs and what the date will be for the next regular billing/payment. Once this dialog box has been completed and OK'd, the transaction will be posted in the current period and will be placed on the memorized transaction list (see Figure 5-9).

To use a memorized transaction in the next period, you simply select "memorized transactions" from the "lists" menu in QuickBooks, and a list like that in Figure 5-9 will appear. You simply highlight the transaction you wish to use and click the "use" icon. You can then adjust the date and amount if you need to or edit it in any other way you see fit. You then click on "save" or "post." Very little data entry is required when you use these memorized transactions—it's quick and easy. Most AP packages offer a similar method for storing and using recurring transactions. See Chapter 3 for an example from One-Write Plus.

Figure 5-9: *Memorized transactions list*

Transaction Name	Type	Source Account	Amount	Frequency	Auto	Next Date
◆ 941 tax deposit	Liability Che	Checking	0.00	Monthly		01/15/96
◆ Fleisher Masonry	Bill	Accounts Payable	145.60	Monthly		01/15/96
◆ **Monthly overhead**	**Group**			**Monthly**		**12/25/95**
◆ Gas & Electric	Check	Checking	0.00			
◆ Health Insurance	Liability Che	Checking	312.00			
◆ Rent	Check	Checking	900.00			
◆ Telephone	Check	Checking	0.00			
◆ Water	Check	Checking	0.00			
◆ State payroll tax deposit	Liability Che	Checking	0.00	Monthly		01/12/96
◆ Workers' Comp	Check	Checking	0.00	Monthly		01/15/96

Memorized Transaction List

[Use] [Edit] [New Group]

Managing Credit Card Purchases

It seems that all small businesses make liberal use of their credit cards to finance purchases. All accounting software packages have procedures for helping you track these charges, but QuickBooks does an especially good job of describing this in their user's manual and provides a menu item titled, "enter credit card charges." Peachtree offers little help on tracking credit cards, and the One-Write Plus procedure is quite convoluted. So here is a quick view of the QuickBooks procedure. After setting up a liability account for your credit card company (e.g., VISA-CitiBank payable), you enter each credit card charge as it occurs on the "enter credit card charges" screen, which is very similar to the "enter bills" screen of Figure 5-5. You can assign the charge to expenses or to inventory items and can even apply it to an open purchase order. This transaction will result in a debit (increase) to asset or expense accounts and a credit (increase) in the credit card liability account "VISA-CitiBank Payable."

When you receive your credit card statement, you select the "reconcile credit card" feature to match the items on that statement to the charge items you have already entered (they appear on a list on-screen). Enter any missing items and the service/finance charge for the period. QuickBooks then gives you the choice of writing a check for the balance due or entering a bill (like all other AP bills) for later payment. When the payment is actually issued, the computer will debit (decrease) the credit card payable account and credit (decrease) cash.

Handling Voids

We are all human, which means we all make mistakes and sometimes need to void checks. In general, the process of voiding a check transaction within an AP system means that you will want to mark the payment transaction (the check) as VOID and remove the amounts that had been posted to the asset, expense, and vendor accounts. Proper accounting procedure demands that the check number and payee should still appear in your records so there is no question that the item was appropriately voided rather than that a missing check was fraudulently used.

In Peachtree, there is a "void checks" menu item under the "tasks" menu. In One-Write Plus, you will find a "void" icon at the top of all transaction screens. In QuickBooks, you can select "void" from the "edit" menu whenever there is a transaction showing on screen. Once you select this menu item in Peachtree, you will be presented with a list of checks that were written in the current period. You simply highlight the check you wish to void and select the "void" button. The current date appears as the suggested void date (you can overtype this date), and when you give the OK, the void is posted to all appropriate accounts. When you print a check register, you will see that both the original check and the void check (e.g., check 108 and check 108V) appear on this list. In One-Write Plus, the original check remains on the check list, but with a zero dollar amount and the word "VOID" next to the vendor name. Similarly, both the original payment and the voided payment appear in the vendor record and in the cash payments journal.

Debit Memos and Adjustments

Debit memos are notifications from your vendors, or documents that you issue yourself, indicating that an adjustment is to be made to an accounts payable (vendor) account. For example, if you return goods, or receive an adjustment for lack of service or quality, you would want your accounts payable obligation to be reduced (that is it would be decreased—a debit, which is why it is called a debit memo.) In most accounting packages, you can enter this transaction in the "purchases" entry screen by simply identifying the vendor and entering a negative (or minus) amount for the transaction. If inventory items are involved, you may have to enter negative quantities; the computer will look up the item unit price and display the total negative amount, which you could overtype if there was a price change. Some packages have a separate data entry screen for entering debit memos and adjustments, but they require the same data items as a purchase transaction.

To link a return/adjustment with the original purchase, use the same invoice number as the original purchase. If the software will not allow duplicate invoice numbers, then try adding a few characters. For example, if the original invoice was 1312, enter 1312ad for the adjustment transaction.

Summary of Accounts Payable Transactions

Although I have described the posting results for each type of AP transaction throughout this chapter, it may be helpful for you to see these transactions summarized in one place. I hope you will use the following as a reference tool. To summarize:

Purchases on Account:
- cause a debit (increase) to an asset or expense
- and a credit (increase) to accounts payable

Payments on Account:
- cause a debit (decrease) to accounts payable
- and a credit (decrease) to cash

Direct Check Payments:
- cause a debit (increase) to asset or expense
- and a credit (decrease) to cash

Returns/Adjustments:
- cause a debit (decrease) to accounts payable
- and a credit (decrease) to the asset or expense

All of these accounts are maintained as separate records in the general ledger, and the expense accounts are, of course, used to determine net income. The ending balance in the accounts payable account in the general ledger will match (or balance to) the total of all the ending balances in the accounts payable vendor accounts.

Saving and Backing Up Your Data

Once again, the process of backing up your accounting data is so important that it should not be left to chance. All businesses should make backup copies of data files every day! So just another reminder—use the backup procedure that is built into the software, or develop your own—*but do it!* Most packages will provide a menu item for this procedure, so you have no excuse to neglect this task. The procedure and an illustration of the backup process was illustrated in Chapter 2, "Choosing and Using Accounting Software."

Chapter Six

Accounts Payable Reports

The Importance of Timely Accounts Payable Reports

Accounts payable (AP) systems are capable of producing numerous reports; some are absolutely necessary, some are optionally helpful, and some are frills. The title of a report does not usually do justice to the importance of its content or its purpose, and different software publishers produce widely different variations on the same report. With most contemporary accounting software, you also have the ability to customize any existing reports in a way that suits you. It is up to you to choose which reports to print regularly and retain for historical records. You need a basic understanding of these reports in order to make the choices that fit your business needs.

A good example of a very necessary and helpful accounts payable report is the printout of the vendor ledger. This listing would contain the details of all current transactions with your vendors and, of course, would report the ending balance owed on a specific date. With this report, the business manager is able to plan for future payments, answer queries from vendors on account activity, and ensure that proper attention is being paid to your most important suppliers.

This chapter describes some of the reports that are available from accounts payable (AP) software. The goal here is to help you understand what is available as AP output in order to make the best use of the management information that is provided.

Getting the Printed Results

Most accounting software packages will have a "reports" icon or menu with "general ledger, accounts payable, accounts receivable, and payroll" as report categories within that menu. QuickBooks places the printing of lists and forms under the "file, print" menu in addition to having the traditional "reports" menu. One-Write Plus hides a "print" selection under the "entries" menu, which leads to the printing of checks, invoices, statements, labels, etc. When you select "accounts payable" reports or "vendor" reports, you will be faced with many report choices. Here are the most common ones:

- cash payments journal
- cash requirements report (or cash flow forecast)
- check register
- checks (some with remittance advice)
- purchase orders and reports
- purchases journal
- vendor lists
- vendor ledger
- vendor mailing labels
- 1099 Forms

Make your choice from the reports list, and you will probably be asked for some customizing choices like the period of time to include, the column headings you prefer, and a host of other options, depending on the sophistication of your accounting package. Most software allows you to "filter" reports, i.e., you can specify criteria for what is to be included, like specific types of transactions or a selected set of vendors. You should be able to specify whether you want the reports displayed on-screen or printed immediately. Peachtree shows the reports on-screen first (this is a default setting that you can alter if you choose to), and from the displayed report, you can click on a "print" icon; the same is true in One-Write Plus and QuickBooks. QuickBooks even allows you to zoom in on crowded reports that are difficult to view on-screen. You probably won't need all of the reports offered, so let's talk about the purpose of each.

Absolutely Necessary Reports

The printed results of processing accomplished by your computer is called the audit trail (introduced in Chapter 3). The accounts payable audit trail includes source documents, such as the invoices you receive from your vendors, but most importantly, it is comprised of the reports that give evidence of what transactions were recorded and the financial status that resulted. For example, when checks are written, a check register provides the "trail" that can be used to trace the purpose of each check back to a specific transaction.

The AP audit trail should include a check register, purchases journal, cash payments journal, vendor ledger, and 1099 Forms or reports at a minimum. A cash requirements report, or cash flow forecast, is also high on the usefulness list. Many other reports are usually available at a keystroke, some of which are described later in this chapter.

Necessary for Your Vendors

Checks

The production of accurate and timely checks to pay your suppliers was probably one of the first reasons why you wanted an automated accounting system. The check is a negotiable instrument that may be cashed, or it may be deposited with a bank to withdraw funds from your account and pay them to the payee named on the check. Figure 6-1 provides an example: the check is preprinted with your company name, check number, bank, and account number in magnetic coded form—the computer prints the date, payee, amount (in both numeric and text form) and indication of purpose ("memo").

Figure 6-1: *Sample remittance advice check*

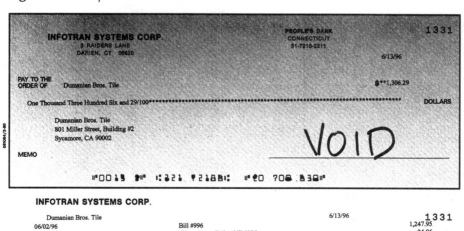

INFOTRAN SYSTEMS CORP.

Dumanian Bros. Tile		6/13/96	1331
06/02/96	Bill #996		1,247.95
06/02/96	Discount applied to bill #996		-24.96
06/03/96	Bill #998		85.00
06/03/96	Discount applied to bill #998		-1.70

Most business software produces checks with a perforated tear-off section, called the remittance advice; this is a short form that describes the reason for the check, such as purchase order numbers, vendor invoice numbers, discounts taken, and the details of how the amount of the check was calculated. I have used the plural form in the previous sentence because you may sometimes want to write a check for a total amount that encompasses several purchases or services provided on several dates. Some software packages call this a voucher check. The remittance advice at the bottom of Figure 6-1 lists the bills the check is paying and the discounts the issuer is claiming.

Your AP software will also provide you with the option of printing checks as you write them or printing them as a batch. For example, One-Write Plus has a "print" icon (a tiny printer with a form sticking out of it) at the top of the "write checks" screen so that you can print each check as you enter it. Alternatively, you can "save" the check transactions and select "entries, print, checks" to print a batch of checks later.

You will also have the option of printing checks in various sizes and formats (7" checks with voucher, 7" without voucher, 9" checks in various formats, two to a page, three to a page, etc.) QuickBooks even has an option called "partial page checks" that allows you to use up a page of laser checks where the first check had been torn off and only one check remains.

Note that even if checks are written manually, you probably want to record the basic transaction data for the payment in your software. If you do this, you will have to print the checks on plain paper, or they will remain in the print queue forever! It is assumed in this chapter that you produce the checks automatically using the AP software, but the rest of this chapter applies whether you prepare checks manually or automatically.

Necessary for Operational Control

Check Registers

The internal "proof of payment" for an expenditure usually rests with the check register. Small companies do not produce and retain a copy of every single check, and most banks are no longer returning canceled checks with the monthly bank statement, so a list of checks is needed. The check register can be produced for any specified period of time (a week, a month, two months, etc.) and would list each check written by check number, date, payee, and net amount of the check. Figure 6-2 provides you with a sample check register from One-Write Plus. Since this report does not contain any detail about the expense accounts to be charged, or whether discounts were taken, the cash payments journal (later in this chapter) should also be printed once per month. After you read the description of the cash payments journal, compare it to your own cash payments journal and decide whether it might also serve as a check register. If your cash payments journal lists check numbers and is in order by date, it may double as a check register. If your business is very small, you can probably get along with one or the other.

Figure 6-2: *Sample check register*

			The Kite Store **CHECK REGISTER** Checking Account 3/1/96 To 3/31/96	
REF NO	**DATE**	**TT**	**DESCRIPTION**	**DIST. AMOUN**
00000246	03/15/96	EC	Mike Jones	-273.91
00000247	03/15/96	EC	Michelle Smith	-105.29
00000248	03/15/96	EC	Frank Williams	-825.98
00000249	03/29/96	EC	Mike Jones	-376.30
00000250	03/29/96	EC	Michelle Smith	-191.52
00000251	03/29/96	EC	Frank Williams	-825.98
00000252	03/23/96	VC	*VOID*Public Utilities Corp.	0.00
00000253	03/23/96	VC	*VOID*North American Telephone	0.00
00000254	03/25/96	VC	Public Utilities Corp.	-364.55

(this is a partial report)

The check register is used in the bank reconciliation process (for identifying and marking canceled checks to determine which checks are still outstanding) and for controlling the sequencing of checks. All check numbers should be accounted for; thus the check register should be in check number sequence and contain voided checks, as well as cashed checks, with no check numbers missing. These last two purposes are important internal control functions.

Accounts Payable Ledger (the Vendor Ledger)

The accounts payable ledger would list, for each vendor, the previous period balance owed, the details of all current transactions, and the ending balance owed on a specific date. With this report, the business manager is able to plan for future payments, answer queries from vendors on account activity, and ensure that proper attention is being paid to your most important suppliers. Printing of this report constitutes the minimum "audit trail" for an accounts payable system. As you can see from Figure 6-3, the QuickBooks vendor ledger report would present columns for vendor name (and/or ID # if you prefer), date, transaction number, transaction amount as a debit or credit, and a running balance.

Figure 6-3: *Vendor ledger—detailed listing*

	Rock Castle Construction				
	Vendor Balance Detail				
	4th Quarter 1995				
Type	**Date**	**Num**	**Debit**	**Credit**	**Balance**
Hennessy Metal					500.00
Bill Pmt -Check	10/10/95	830	500.00		0.00
Bill	11/1/95			3,100.00	3,100.00
Bill Pmt -Check	11/29/95	872	3,100.00		0.00
Bill	12/1/95			250.00	250.00
Total Hennessy Metal			3,600.00	3,350.00	250.00
Heywood Appliances					0.00
Bill	10/2/95			1,855.00	1,855.00
Bill Pmt -Check	10/11/95	833	1,817.90		37.10
Discount	10/11/95	833	37.10		0.00
Bill	11/27/95			2,180.00	2,180.00
Total Heywood Appliances			1,855.00	4,035.00	2,180.00
Luxton Flooring					3,000.00
Bill	10/10/95			1,500.00	4,500.00
Bill Pmt -Check	10/19/95	840	3,000.00		1,500.00
Bill Pmt -Check	11/3/95	852	1,500.00		0.00
Bill	11/25/95			5,600.00	5,600.00
Bill	12/9/95			3,000.00	8,600.00
Total Luxton Flooring			4,500.00	10,100.00	8,600.00

(this is a partial report)

The debits to these accounts are usually your check payments, and the credits are usually new purchases. Please note that this report does not include the GL account numbers used in the transaction; any transaction in the vendor ledger can be traced to its source by use of the transaction type, (e.g., "bill" refers to a purchase invoice and "bill pmt-check" refers to a vendor check). The vendor ledger report should always include a grand total at the bottom of the report, which represents the total of all monies owed by all vendors combined (not shown in this figure). This total amount should be compared with the ending balance in the accounts payable account in the general ledger for the same date. Ensuring that these two figures are in balance is called "reconciling accounts payable" and is considered part of good internal control procedures.

Vendor Ledger Summary Report

The vendor ledger report just described would be considered to be a detailed report. You could also print the vendor ledger in summary form; with just the vendor name and the ending balance at a specific date. This would be titled the schedule of accounts payable and is not often used in an automated system because it provides no references to trace current transactions.

Transaction Journals

Since purchase and payment transactions are the two feeders to an AP system, the purchases journal and the cash payments journal would contain the bulk of transactions that are posted (copied) to the AP ledger. In order to have a printed history of the transactions that caused vendor balances to increase or decrease, it is imperative to print both of these journals.

Purchases Journal

The purchases journal is usually arranged in date order and lists a vendor name and/or ID, a purchase invoice number, the accounts and amounts debited, accounts and amounts credited, and a grand total. An example from One-Write Plus is shown in Figure 6-4. Notice that most transactions in this journal include a credit (increase) to accounts payable (account 2000 in the figure), because those are purchases on account. The debits range from debits to supplies and advertising expense to debits to purchases. Each line in this journal can be traced to the vendor accounts and to the general ledger accounts.

Figure 6-4: *Sample purchases journal*

	The Kite Store			
	VENDOR PURCHASE JOURNAL			
	3/1/96 TO 3/31/96			
<u>DATE</u>	<u>TT</u> <u>ID</u> <u>NAME</u>		<u>REF NO</u>	<u>AMOUNT</u>
03/04/96	VI STRINGS Strings & Things		00003252	837.64
	6440 Supplies Expense		837.64 dr	
	2000 Accounts Payable		837.64 dr	
03/04/96	VI ACCPRINT Accurate Printing Company		00000864	364.85
	5160 Brochures and Catalogs		364.85 dr	
	2000 Accounts Payable		364.85 cr	
03/04/96	VI ALLSILK All Silk Designs		00008446	325.41
	4310 Purchases		325.41 dr	
	2000 Accounts Payable		324.41 cr	
03/12/96	VI AZSUPPLY A - Z Supply Company		00000548	957.45
	6440 Supplies Expense		957.45 dr	
	2000 Accounts Payable		957.45 cr	
03/12/96	VI CREATADD Creative Advertising Company	00849278		984.86
	5100 Advertising		984.86 dr	
	2000 Accounts Payable		984.86 cr	

(this is a partial report)

Cash Payments Journal

The cash payments journal (sometimes called a cash disbursement journal) is also printed in date order and contains the same basic columns as the purchases journal. Figure 6-5 provides a sample cash disbursements journal from Peachtree. The importance of this report can be seen in the listing of account IDs for each transaction; this is where you see the full effect of the transaction. Each line in this journal can be traced to the vendor accounts and to the general ledger accounts. For example, the first transaction in Figure 6-5 shows a debit (decrease) to accounts payable, account 22000, and a credit (decrease) to cash, account 10100. The second transaction is a direct payment (no purchase invoice was entered in the purchases journal) from cash, account 10100, and is charged to rent expense, account 68000.

Figure 6-5: *Sample cash disbursements journal*

			JAN'S JUMPING SERVICE		
			Cash Disbursements Journal		
			For the Period From Jan1, 1994 to Jan 31, 1994		
Date	Account ID	Check #	Line Description	Debit Amount	Credit Amount
1/1/94	22000	101	Invoice: 99991	123.60	
	10100		JEAN GUTMANN		123.60
1/2/94	68000		Monthly Rent at 94 Maine Street	600.00	
	10100		OFFICE SPACE MGMT SERVICES		600.00
1/3/94	61300		Monthly Liability Premium	148.00	
	10100		MORSE, PAYSON & NOYES INS.		148.00
1/31/94	22000	102	Invoice:10001	400.00	
	10100		SKY HIGH JUMP EQUIPMENT		400.00
1/31/94	22000	102V	Invoice:10001		400.00
	10100		SKY HIGH JUMP EQUIPMENT	400.00	

You should also notice the void transaction of January 31—both the original check 102, and a void check 102V appear on that date. This audit trail shows the real situation here instead of neglecting to show check 102 because it was torn up and discarded.

Other Useful Accounts Payable Reports

Cash Requirements Report

The cash requirements report (Peachtree) alerts you to upcoming required payments. The cash requirements report is sometimes called the open invoice report (One-Write Plus) because it shows the purchase invoices that you have previously entered but for which you have not yet written a check. Please recall that the AP ledger shows what has been purchased and already paid for; you also need to know what is left to be paid. In other words, the total shown on the cash requirements report is the amount that would be required in your checking account if you were to pay all outstanding bills. Refer to Figure 6-6 for a sample Cash Requirements Report. When you select this Peachtree report you can even specify the period of the report so you can make your plans for what to pay within the next few months, weeks, or even the next few days.

In Chapter 5, the activity of writing checks for previously scheduled purchase invoices was illustrated. Do you recall from that presentation that in Peachtree,

Figure 6-6: *Sample cash requirements report*

Bellweather Cleaning Services Cash Requirements As of Apr 30, 1995						
Vendor	Invoice No	Date	Date Due	Amount Due	Disc Amt	Net to Pay
Davis Paper Supply	6001	1/9/95	2/11/95	527.70	10.55	517.15
	30199-10	2/13/95	3/15/95	206.50	4.13	202.37
Davis Paper Supply				**734.20**		**719.52**
Jade & Assoc.	2005	1/3/95	2/2/95	950.00	19.00	931.00
	56889	3/24/95	4/23/95	320.00	6.40	313.60
	98698	3/28/95	4/27/95	2,400.00	48.00	2,352.00
Jade & Assoc.				**3,670.00**		**3,596.60**

(this is a partial report)

when you display the payments screen and specify a vendor, the currently outstanding invoices for that vendor will show up on a folder tab at the bottom of the screen. To pay one of the outstanding invoices, you simply highlight that invoice and type in the amount to pay (which could be the full amount or a partial payment). I suggest that the cash requirements report is an optional report because the information contained in that report can also be found on the payments screen for each vendor. But if you want to plan for upcoming payments as a group, and need to know how much cash is required to make those payments, this is a good report to print, as-needed or on a regular basis.

Vendor Master List

The vendor master list provides a hard copy list of all the data on file for each vendor. This listing will present in tabular format all the fields that you see on the "maintain vendors" input screen. Figure 6-7 provides an example from One-Write Plus. This listing includes such items as vendor ID code, vendor name, contact name, address, various phone numbers, payment terms, 1099 code, default expense account numbers, and the current balance with this customer. The vendor master list is commonly used to provide a printed list of the current computer file that can be used to make notations for changes such as change of address or phone number or contact person. Some businesses use this, along with a customer master list, for a quick reference phone book. It would not be necessary to print this report more than a few times per year, as long as the details of the AP ledger are printed monthly.

Figure 6-7: *Sample vendor master list*

The Kite Store
VENDOR CARD REPORT

VENDOR ID: ALLSILK   **CATEGORY: Inventory**

ADDRESS: **PURCHASES:**
All Silk Designs   Expense Account: 4310 Purchases
3450 Oregon Avenue   Vendor Account #: 22-1947
Burbank, CA 90000   Payment Terms: 2% 10 Net 30
USA

Phone: (374) 582-9523 x1221   Fax: (374) 582-3745
Contact:

OPTIONS:
Always Take Discount: No   1099 Vendor: No
Hold Transactions: No   Occasional: No
Inactive: No   Taxpayer EIN:

                                          VENDOR BALANCE: 210.66

COMMENTS:

VENDOR HISTORY

DATE	TT	REF NO	DUE DATE	H	AMOUNT	OPEN BALANCE	DISC	DISC AVAIL
01/03/96	VI	00027346	02/02/96		475.32	0.00	01/13	9.51
01/03/96	VI	00062384	02/02/96		374.92	296.49	01/13	7.50
02/06/96	VI	00062341	03/07/96		83.74	5.31	02/16	1.67
02/16/96	VP	00000347			-978.44	503.12		0.00

Mailing Labels

Any file within an accounting package that contains names and addresses can be printed in the form of mailing labels. Small businesses don't very often find it necessary to print a complete set of vendor mailing labels—it is far easier to buy window envelopes for sending vendor checks than it is to print one label at a time by pointing to it in the vendor reports specifications. You will most likely have to print all vendors, or a class of vendors, on the mailing labels. But you will have choices concerning the type and size of the labels, and will probably want to print a set of these periodically to use for special correspondence with vendors such as advertising, sales, brochures, etc.

Accounts Payable Graphs

Purchase and payment transactions that can be grouped by account or vendor have the potential for being presented in graphic form. Peachtree and QuickBooks provide graph output for aged payables (vendor balances by due date). One-Write Plus offers no graphs. Graphs are generally not as useful, or as widely used, in the area of accounts payable as they are in general ledger, accounts receivable, and inventory. An example of an aged payables graph from QuickBooks appears in Figure 6-8. You can see from this graph that of the total amount due to be paid ($32,320.00), about $12,000 is current (not yet due), and about $20,000 is overdue by up to thirty days. The pie graph section shows what percentage of the total is owed to which vendors. The only fault with this approach is that not all obligations due in 30 to 120 days have been entered into accounts payable as data; for example, your recurring rent and insurance payments are not included in this payables total.

Figure 6-8: *Sample payables graph*

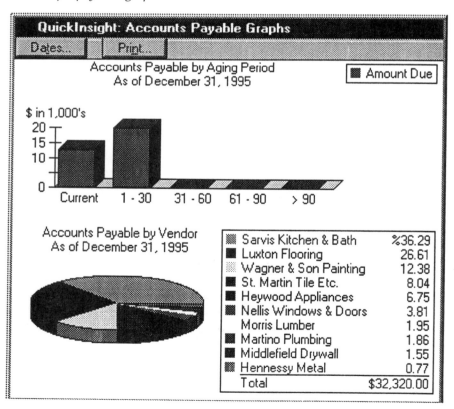

Purchase Orders and Reports

Peachtree and QuickBooks have the capacity to accept input for, and print, purchase orders. Not many low-end packages have this feature. Purchase orders are not posted as transactions in the accounting system, but are noted in the vendor ledger with the amount not accumulated in the balance owed until the invoice is received. If you enter data for purchase orders, you would, of course, be able to print the purchase orders themselves and print a detailed listing of the purchase orders. This is an advanced procedure that should be researched in your software user's manual.

Complying with the Law

Form 1099—Miscellaneous Income

If you make payments to independent contractors (e.g., have the office painted by a local painter), you do not deduct payroll taxes from the gross amount you pay to them. Because they are obligated by income tax laws to report all of their own income and pay taxes on it, they and the government rely on a Form 1099 for the official reporting of this income. The IRS calls this miscellaneous income. At the end of each year, you are obligated to prepare and send 1099s to all contractors and subcontractors to whom you paid more than $600.

Your AP software will assist you in doing this as long as you have coded your vendors in such a way that the computer can pick out the vendors who need this form. In figure 6-7 from the One-Write Plus vendor master file, you can see a field at the bottom right where you indicate whether a vendor is a "1099 vendor." At the end of your accounting year, you would select "1099 Forms" from the "entries, print, tax forms" menu items. A 1099 Form will print for each of the identified vendors who received more than $600 from you. You may choose to print these on plain paper and then manually fill out the 1099 Form provided by the government, or you can buy the forms on continuous feed (or laser page) paper and fiddle with the printer alignment until you get the forms filled in correctly. A 1099 Form example printed by One-Write Plus is shown in Figure 6-9.

Figure 6-9: *Sample 1099 Form*

```
      9595          ☐ VOID    ☐ CORRECTED
┌─────────────────────────────────────┬──────────────────────┬─────────────────────┬────────────────────┐
│ PAYER'S name, street address, city,  │ 1 Rents              │ OMB No. 1545-0115   │                    │
│ state, and ZIP code                  │ $                    │                     │                    │
│ The Kite Store                       ├──────────────────────┤                     │                    │
│ 119 Breezy Avenue                    │ 2 Royalties          │    19⑨95            │ Miscellaneous      │
│ P.O. Box 2                           │ $                    │                     │ Income             │
│ Windswept, MA 00000                  ├──────────────────────┤                     │                    │
│                                      │ 3 Other income       │ Form 1099-MISC      │                    │
│                                      │ $                    │                     │                    │
├──────────────────┬───────────────────┼──────────────────────┼─────────────────────┼────────────────────┤
│ PAYER'S Federal  │ RECIPIENT'S       │ 4 Federal income tax │ 5 Fishing boat      │     Copy A         │
│ identification   │ identification    │   withheld           │   proceeds          │                    │
│ number           │ number            │ $                    │ $                   │      For           │
├──────────────────┴───────────────────┼──────────────────────┼─────────────────────┤ Internal Revenue   │
│ RECIPIENT'S name                      │ 6 Medical and health │ 7 Nonemployee       │ Service Center     │
│ All Silk Designs                      │   care payments      │   compensation      │                    │
│                                       │ $                    │ $    1280.24        │ File with Form 1096.│
│                                       ├──────────────────────┼─────────────────────┼────────────────────┤
│                                       │ 8 Substitute         │ 9 Payer made direct │ For Paperwork      │
│                                       │   payments in lieu of│   sales of $5,000 or│ Reduction Act      │
│ Street address (including apt. no.)   │   dividends or       │   more of consumer  │ Notice and         │
│ 3450 Oregon Avenue                    │   interest           │   products to a     │ instructions for   │
│                                       │ $                    │   buyer (recipient) │ completing this form,│
├───────────────────────────────────────┼──────────────────────┤   for resale ▶  ☐   │ see Instructions for│
│ City, state, and ZIP code             │ 10 Crop insurance    │ 11 State income tax │ Forms 1099, 1098,  │
│ Burbank, CA 90000                     │    proceeds          │    withheld         │ 5498, and W-2G.    │
│                                       │ $                    │ $                   │                    │
├───────────────────────────────────────┼──────────────────────┴─────────────────────┤                    │
│ Account number (optional)             │ 2nd TIN Not. 12 State/Payer's state number   │                    │
│                                       │ ☐                                            │                    │
└───────────────────────────────────────┴──────────────────────────────────────────────┴────────────────────┘
 Form 1099-MISC              Cat. No. 14425J        Department of the Treasury - Internal Revenue Service
```

Paying Sales Taxes

QuickBooks takes the unique approach to your sales tax obligations that it is an accounts payable function, even though your obligation to pay sales taxes comes from the sales process of earning revenue. On the QuickBooks "tasks" menu, you will find "pay sales taxes" grouped with accounts payable tasks. On the accounts payable reports menu, you will find a sales tax report. This is worth mentioning here because this makes it very easy to find and pay the right amount of sales taxes. QuickBooks displays the year-to-date sales tax amounts owed to various taxing authorities, so all you have to do is select the items in a manner similar to paying an invoice due from one of your vendors. Sales taxes and a sales tax reports will be discussed in more detail in Chapters 7 and 8.

What to Save/What to Ignore

When you first install an accounting system, it is a good idea to experiment with all the various reports that each module provides. You will need to match the information provided on the reports with your needs and personal preferences. Try to keep in mind that your business history is represented by your accounting reports, and choose among the available reports with "comparability" in mind. In other words, print reports on a periodic basis that can be compared to previous periods for reasonableness, growth, and general business health. My recommendation for the minimum set of AP reports to be printed and filed each period in a book or folder is:

- the check register
- the detailed vendor ledger listing
- the purchases journal
- the cash payments journal

If you pay contractors and subcontractors, you are also required by law to print, save, and submit to both the payee and the IRS, the 1099 Form.

If you sell services only and do not deal in materials, you can definitely forgo purchase orders and purchase activity reports. If your volume of AP transactions is small, you can probably skip the check register and use the cash payments journal in its place (as long as the Journal includes check numbers). I have never found much use for AP graphs, but I need a cash requirements report each month to estimate my cash needs. Again, analyze your needs, and decide what reports are best for your business, keeping your growth in mind.

Exporting Accounts Payable Reports to Other Software

Please refer to the "Exporting Output to Other Software" section in Chapter 4 for a general introduction to this feature. This is a rather advanced function, but sometimes it would be helpful to use your vendor balances or a copy of your vendor master list in your spreadsheet or word processing software. For example, you might be writing a report to include with a loan application that asks you to list each of your current payables greater than $500 by vendor with a lump sum for the vendors under $500. Once you export your vendor list with ending balances to a spreadsheet, you can delete the lines with amounts under $500, enter the total of those amounts in a cell at the bottom of the list, and write a formula to calculate the overall total. Figure 6-10 provides an example spreadsheet using Quattro Pro with data imported from QuickBooks.

Figure 6-10: *Spreadsheet using accounts payable data*

	A	B	C
	APBALS.WB2		
1	FOR CITIBANK LOAN APPLICATION - FROM MACADAMIA CONSTRUCTION		
2			
3	ACCOUNTS PAYABLE BALANCES OVER $500 AS OF JUNE 15, 1996		
4			
5	VENDOR:	AMOUNT OWED:	
6	Heywood Appliances	$2,180.00	
7	Luxton Flooring	$8,600.00	
8	Martino Plumbing	$600.00	
9	Nellis Windows & Doors	$1,230.00	
10	Sarvis Kitchen & Bath	$11,730.00	
11	St. Martin Tile Etc.	$2,600.00	
12	Wagner & Son Painting	$4,000.00	
13	All Other Vendors	$895.60	
14			
15	TOTAL	$31,835.60	
16			

The process for accomplishing this task generally involves these steps:

1. Display and/or print the report in AP that most closely resembles the data you want in your spreadsheet or word processor.

2. Select the "export" command from the print options.

3. Verify what data to export, what type of export file to create (e.g., a plain text file, a tab delimited data file, or a specific spreadsheet file), and where to store it (e.g., the A: drive, or a special subdirectory on C:).

4. Open your spreadsheet or word processor software and use the appropriate "file, import," "file, open," "file, retrieve," or "tools, import" commands to open the file saved in step three.

Refer to your user's manual for both the accounting package and the other software package for help in importing and exporting files. Windows 95 (Microsoft Corporation) is making it easier for these two types of packages to use the same files.

Chapter Seven

Sales and Accounts Receivable

Introduction to Sales and Accounts Receivable Functions

In contemporary business exchanges, the use of credit has become so common-place that no accounting software would be worth its cost unless it included the ability to record, report, and manage credit sale transactions. This ability is enhanced by the maintenance of detailed customer records and management reports that include a list of customer balances, as well as a schedule of aged receivables that allows the follow-up of payment reminders and collection letters. The "squeaky wheel gets the grease": constant reminders to customers who are overdue on account result in higher collection rates and an improved company financial picture.

When a business sells goods or services, it either receives cash for the sale, or it accepts a promise to pay that creates an account receivable (AR) on its records. A cash sale is recorded by increasing the cash account and increasing a revenue account (such as sales or book sales or fees earned or service revenue). A sale on account is recorded by increasing the accounts receivable account and increasing one of the revenue accounts mentioned above.

If inventory is being sold under either of the above scenarios, the inventory account would also be decreased while a cost of goods sold account (an expense of doing business) is increased for reporting the items sold on an income statement. When payment is received for goods or services sold on account, the accounts receivable account is then decreased and cash is increased.

Note: The accrual method of accounting is assumed in the discussions in this chapter. See Chapter 3 for an explanation of accrual basis accounting.

This chapter is devoted to the procedures commonly used to record the sales and accounts receivable transactions just described, and to help you understand what a computer system does with this data. The next chapter is devoted to the production and use of accounts receivable reports to effect better business management.

How an Accounts Receivable System Works

In Figure 7-1, the "Navigation Aid" from the Peachtree display provides a nutshell view of accounts receivable components. Note that sales and receipts are the two major inputs to a receivables system. The sale of goods or services is usually followed by the presentation of a sales invoice to the customer. When payments are received from the customer, these cash receipts are deposited in a checking account. These transactions are recorded in the sales journal and the receipts journal and are then posted (copied) to both the customer accounts and the general ledger accounts. In Peachtree, One-Write Plus, and QuickBooks, the sales journal and cash receipts journal are created automatically by the software during the sales and receipts data entry process.

Figure 7-1: *Navigation aid for accounts receivable from Peachtree*

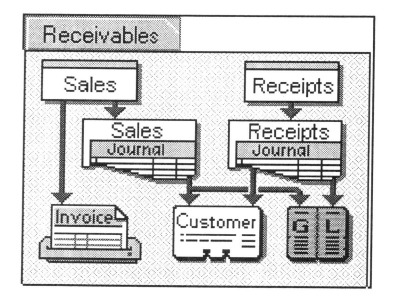

What Goes on inside the Accounts Receivable Module?

A more detailed flowchart of AR elements and procedures is shown in Figure 7-2.

Figure 7-2: *Accounts Receivable (AR) data flow*

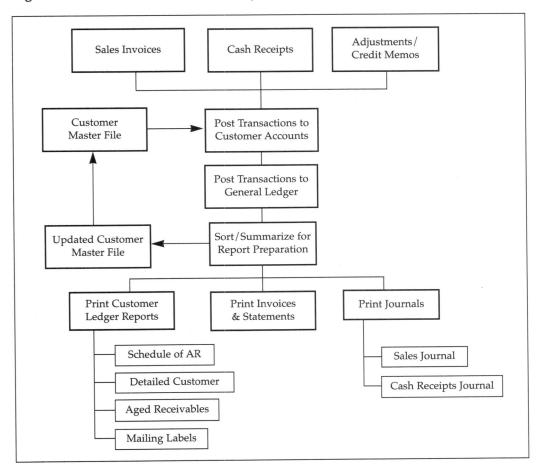

Input

The most common input files and documents for the AR module are:

- customer master file
- sales items master file
- sales invoices

- cash receipts forms
- any credit memos

The customer master file contains the permanent information about customers like addresses, phone numbers, ship-to addresses, selling terms, credit limits, and sales tax information. The sales item master file contains the permanent information about items or categories of service that you sell. Most accounting software, like Peachtree or QuickBooks, allows you to enter sales data directly onto a screen form that resembles a traditional sales invoice. The sales data is linked with a customer master file and an item (or inventory) file in order to automate the process of filling in the form. Cash receipts entries also rely on information in these master files. Occasionally, you may have to adjust one of the above transactions or enter a credit memo for a customer because of returned goods.

Processing

The basic processing that occurs within an AR system includes:

- the calculation of extensions, subtotals, discounts, and totals
- the calculation of sales taxes and finance charges where appropriate
- the posting of sales and receipts to individual customer accounts
- the posting of amounts to appropriate general ledger accounts
- the sorting and summarizing of files for reports

In the blink of an eye, the computer will do any calculations necessary to complete an invoice or cash receipt form; invoice extensions (quantity times price) and discount amounts are always figured accurately. When appropriate, adding sales taxes and applying finance charges are also accurately accomplished. All of the above transactions are then automatically posted (copied) to customer accounts and to various appropriate accounts in the general ledger. Since many reports will be printed by the AR module, the files must be sorted in date order for some, customer name for others, and due date for others. All of these functions constitute the processing that goes on behind the scenes in the AR module.

Output

The most common outputs from an AR system are:

- the customer invoices and statements
- the accounts receivable (customer) ledger listings
- the accounts receivable transaction listings

The most important reason for entering credit sales data into the computer is so that you can produce the "bill" (sales invoice) to present to your customer. The contents of the accounts receivable ledger (sometimes called the customer ledger) is printed and displayed in many formats. The general ledger postings are shown in sales journals, cash receipts journals, and adjustments journals (for credit memos and internal adjustments). Most AR packages also include a mailing label printout. More advanced AR systems might also produce collection and sales analysis reports. These AR reports are covered in more detail in Chapter 8.

The Customer Master File

A master file, first explained in Chapter 3, contains relatively permanent pieces of information that are used repeatedly in the processing of transactions. The customer master file contains customer names and addresses, as well as a variety of items that might include some or all of the following:

- customer code (both alpha and numeric)
- customer name
- customer type (e.g., retail, wholesale, cash-basis, etc.)
- customer address, phone, and fax numbers
- contact person's name
- ship-to/bill-to addresses
- discount and payment terms
- sales taxes (county, state, or rate)
- credit limit
- default general ledger sales account number
- sales rep assigned to that customer
- current balance owed

An example of one record within a customer master file from One-Write Plus is shown in Figure 7-3. Take a careful look at the fields on this screen—these are the standard fields that are maintained for each customer. The only field that might need explaining is the "price code" (shown in the lower right corner). This code is used to indicate the sales price that is paid by this customer. Code 1, the highest price, is paid by retail customers; code 2 is paid by sales contractors; and code 3 is paid by wholesalers. In the inventory item file for this sample company, there are three price levels associated with most items sold.

Figure 7-3: *Sample customer master file record*

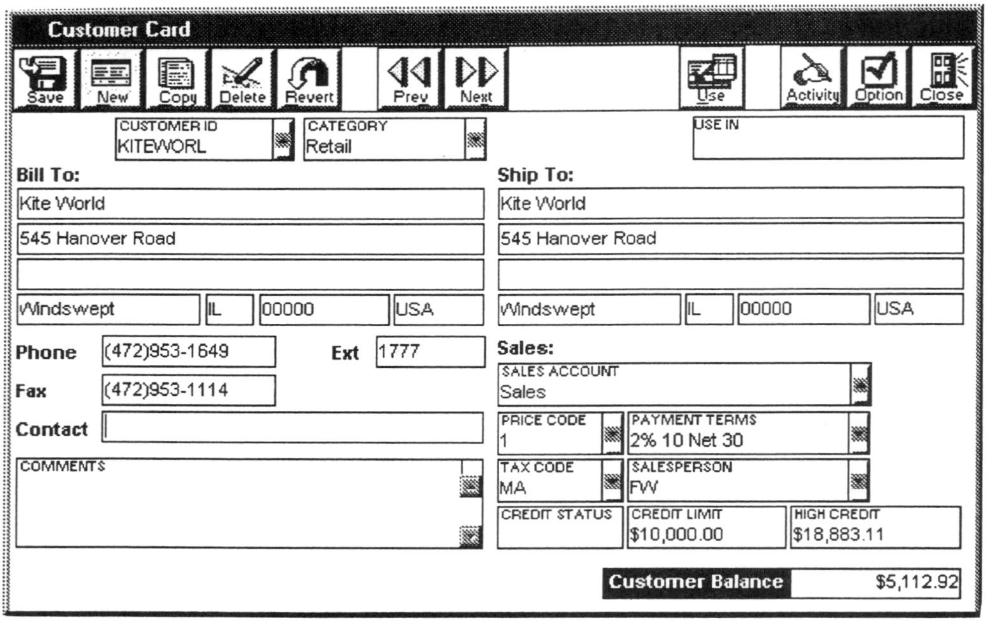

To understand the important role that the customer master file plays in an AR system, let's look at how it is used. When a sales or receipts transaction is being entered, the data entry screen will require that a customer number or customer name be entered. Most AR packages will provide the user with a pop-up table, that is, a list of customers who are already in the customer master file. The user can then select a customer from the list (usually by highlighting the name and clicking), and instantly, all pertinent data from the master file is displayed on the sales or receipt data entry screen. Alternately, some packages allow the user to type the first few letters of a customer's name, and as soon as the computer recognizes the customer, it will provide the rest of the name and any pertinent items from the master file. For example, the user need only type "kit" before the computer would recognize this customer as "Kiteworld" and would display the needed data for this customer.

If the customer being served is not already in the master file, the AR software will notify the user that the customer does not exist and will encourage the user to enter all necessary data to create a new record in the master file. Creating a new customer record during transaction entry for sales or receipts is called master file maintenance "on-the-fly."

Some customer master file maintenance (adding new records, modifying existing records, or deleting unused records) can be done on a periodic basis. If new customers are not entered "on-the-fly," as described in the previous paragraph, a batch of changes may be accumulated over a period of time and then a maintenance procedure is performed on the master file that updates all changed records.

Sales Item Codes Master File

The "sales item codes master file" is created and maintained in a fashion similar to the customer master file. If the business is a service business, this file contains categories of services offered (for example, residential home cleaning, condominium cleaning, office cleaning, etc.) If the business is a merchandising business, this file contains item codes for each of the inventory items sold (for example, speakers, turntables, CD players, etc.) If the AR system is integrated with an inventory module, the inventory item master file serves as the sales item master file. The inventory master file is covered in Chapter 11. A sample sales item master file record from Peachtree is shown in Figure 7-4.

Figure 7-4: *Sample sales item master file record*

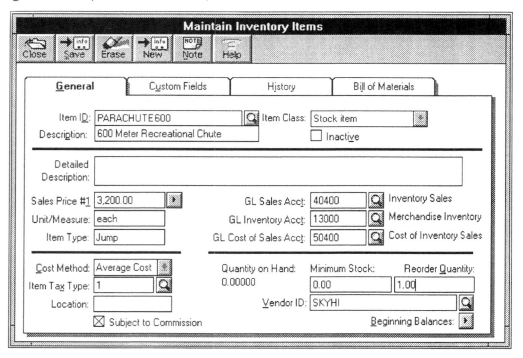

The sales item master file contains sales codes (or inventory item numbers) for each item you sell, with a description of that item, the regular price of the item, the GL revenue account where sales of the item are recorded, and the unit of measurement for the item, if appropriate (for example, per dozen, per gallon, etc.). When a sales invoice transaction is entered, the accounting package will prompt for the item or service that is being sold (a pop-up list of items in the master file is usually available in a separate box on screen, where the user can point and click to choose an item), and the computer will supply the rest of the information on that item. In other words, the description and price will automatically be provided from the sales item master file.

This master file will also hold default general ledger account numbers for the revenue account to be charged when a particular item is sold. If an inventory item is being used, the item will also be associated with a general ledger inventory account number so when an item is sold, the merchandise inventory account can be reduced and the cost of goods sold account increased, as well as a revenue account being increased. Take a minute to search for the GL accounts on the inventory item record (right of center) in Figure 7-4.

Entering Sales Transactions

The sale of goods or services is the lifeblood of all businesses. The sale triggers many other activities in the organization such as inventory management, shipping, billing, collections, revenue analysis, and the determination of net profit. The sale of goods or services causes an increase in business assets (cash or accounts receivable) and an increase in revenue.

In accounting terms, this is recorded as a debit (increase) to accounts receivable or cash, and a credit (increase) to sales revenue. If the sales transaction involves a sale of inventory items, it will also be recorded as a debit (increase) to a cost of sales account, and as a credit (decrease) to inventory. When a sales transaction is entered into your computerized accounting system, the transaction will automatically be recorded in the above named accounts, as well as being recorded in a customer record by the accounts receivable system.

The sales data is normally entered on a data entry screen titled "sales invoice" or "create invoices." A sample of this screen from QuickBooks is shown in Figure 7-5. Please notice that this screen is designed to resemble a traditional handwritten sales invoice. Once the user enters or selects a customer name, the address, date, invoice number, and terms are automatically filled in. The current date is given as a default date, but the user can overtype a new date. A consecutive invoice number is presented, but the user may also overtype this field. Once the user enters a quantity and sales item (this can also be picked from a pop-up list), the computer fills in the description, unit price, and total price for that item. Multiple items on one invoice are entered in the same way, and the total is updated accordingly. If the user wants to include a sales charge for an item not in the master file, it is normally possible to enter the item in the master file as it is being entered on the invoice, and an option is usually provided for "one time only" items. (Is the ability to charge for one time only items important to you? It is if you will often have these items and don't want your pop-up list to be gargantuan.)

Figure 7-5: *Sales invoice transaction entry*

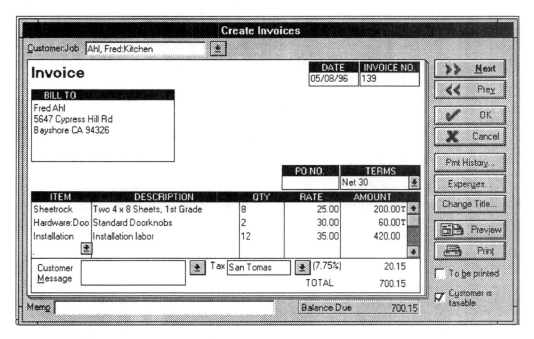

Please notice the "OK" button on the right of Figure 7-5. This command is used to both save and to post (copy) the transaction. In other words, the transaction will be posted to the accounts receivable account and to the appropriate general ledger accounts (described in the first paragraph of this section). Peachtree offers an icon to "post" the transaction, while One-Write Plus uses a "save" icon.

If you want to produce a printed invoice as soon as the sales transaction is entered, simply click on the "print" button (shown in the lower right of Figure 7-5). You can choose to print invoices one by one as you complete the form, or you can choose to print a batch (group) of invoices after you have entered all the invoices for a day or a week. The latter is accomplished in QuickBooks by selecting the "file, print forms, invoices" menu items. A listing of sales transactions is normally displayed or printed by producing a sales journal—covered in detail in the next chapter.

Handling Sales Taxes

The calculation and application of sales taxes will also be handled automatically by the computerized accounting system once you enter your tax municipalities and tax rates. The customer master record usually includes a field that indicates the appropriate sales tax municipality or tax rate for a customer. You can see this in the bottom right area of Figure 7-3, where the tax code has been filled in with "MA." During the software setup procedure, you would name the various states, counties, and cities where you do business and enter a tax rate for each of these. When a sales transaction is entered, the computer uses the sales tax table to "look up" the appropriate tax rate based on the tax code field in the customer master record.

For example, One-Write Plus uses the sales tax card shown in Figure 7-6 to establish the taxing authority (notice the "sales tax ID" and "name" fields) and requires you to specify the tax rate and the GL account where the sales taxes should be accumulated as sales are recorded. The tax rates from these cards are automatically multiplied by the sale amount for taxable items when a sales invoice is entered. The sales tax portion of the sale is recorded by the accounting system as a credit (increase) to sales taxes payable, while accounts receivable is being debited (increased) for the total invoice amount (including the sales tax).

Figure 7-6: *Sample sales tax rates master file*

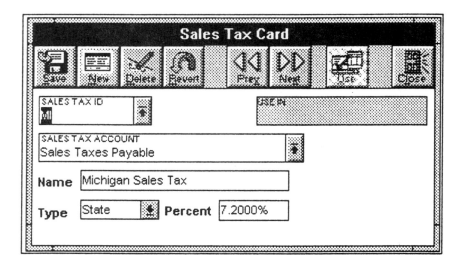

Entering Receipts Transactions

When a payment is received from a customer who previously purchased goods or services on account, the transaction is entered on a receipts transaction screen (like the sample in Figure 7-7 from Peachtree). The display for entering receipts from customers may be quite different, depending on the accounting software used. Some packages present a "deposit ticket" form to parallel your bank deposits. Other packages display the customer ledger and prompt you to identify which customer is paying.

The most convenient display for entering a receipt transaction uses an "open item" approach to maintaining customer records. With the open item approach, each sale transaction is retained in the customer master file until a specific payment has been made for that sale. With this amount of detail stored, the computer can present a list of sales invoices to be marked as "paid" when the customer payment is received. If the payment covers more than one invoice, or is a partial payment, the software will allow the user to mark invoices and override the amount due in order to indicate a partial payment. One-Write Plus, Peachtree, and QuickBooks all employ this open item method of recording customer receipts.

Figure 7-7: *Accounts receivable receipts transaction display*

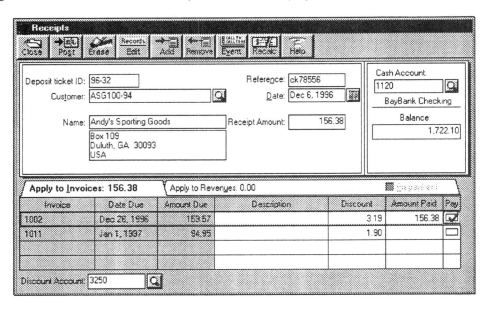

In Peachtree, the receipt of payments from a customer is recorded on the "receipts" screen that is illustrated in Figure 7-7. Once a customer is filled in at the top, the "apply to invoices" tab in the bottom half of the screen displays a list of invoices that are currently outstanding for that customer. With a sales invoice highlighted in the bottom section, the user can click in the "pay" column to add this invoice to the total being received. If a partial payment is being received, the user can move to the "amount paid" field and type in the amount being paid. When the transaction is complete, the "post" icon should be selected. In accounting terms, these transactions are debits to cash and credits to accounts receivable.

The alternative to the open item method is an approach called "balance forward." With this approach, only the ending balance in the customer account is available for review, so a customer payment is applied against the balance due but is not identified with specific invoices. With services like utilities, it is appropriate to use the balance forward method—you will recognize this approach on your electric company bills. With the balance forward method a credit memo is applied against the current balance and not identified with a previous invoice transaction.

A listing of receipts transactions (with their debits and credits) is displayed or printed as a cash receipts journal, which is illustrated in the next chapter.

Cash Sales

When cash is received for a sale of goods or services, no accounts receivable is involved, but it is a good idea to enter the customer name in the customer master file to produce an invoice and keep a record of the customer. The "receipts" transaction screen (again Figure 7-7) is then used to enter the sale, but the "apply to revenue" tab is opened in order to specify the revenue account to which the transaction will be charged. A cash sale results in a debit (increase) to cash and a credit (increase) to sales revenue. If you have emptied your cash register and are recording the total cash sales for the day, the receipts screen would also be used. You can even select two or more revenue accounts to break down the revenue into subcategories. Various revenue categories would be established in the GL chart of accounts based on the business' preference for accumulating sales data (e.g., sporting goods sales, clothing sales, accessories sales.) Some businesses use a customer name of "cash basis" to maintain a ledger record for cash register sales.

Credit Memos and Adjustments

When a customer returns goods or complains about damage or lack of quality, it is often appropriate to issue a credit memo. This means that you have agreed to reduce the customer account balance in accordance with the return or complaint, sometimes called an "allowance." When you reduce accounts receivable, you must credit it; thus the term "credit memo."

In most accounting packages, you can enter this transaction in the "sales invoice" entry screen by simply identifying the customer and entering a negative (or minus) amount for the transaction. If inventory items are involved, you may have to enter negative quantities, and the computer will look up the item unit price and display the total negative amount. Some packages have a separate data entry screen for entering credit memos and adjustments but they require much the same data items as a sales invoice transaction. Once the negative sales invoice is complete, you should access the "receipts" screen of Figure 7-7 to apply the negative invoice to the original invoice for that customer.

To link a return with the original sale, it is a good idea to use the same invoice number as the original sale. If the software will not allow duplicate invoice numbers, try adding a few characters. For example, if the original invoice was 4056, enter "4056cr" for the return transaction.

When you provide a cash refund to a customer, the transaction would be recorded on the "payments" screen, which was described in Chapter 5. At that time, you would specify a revenue account that will be debited (decreased) as cash is automatically credited (decreased) when a check is written.

Another type of adjustment is required when you determine that a customer account has "gone bad." Accounting principles dictate that the customer balance be written off. This type of adjustment uses a bad debt expense account and requires the advice of your accountant, so I won't risk discussing it inadequately here.

Summary of Accounts Receivable Posting

The word posting in accounts receivable refers to the process of copying all parts of the sales and receipts transactions into the appropriate customer and general ledger accounts. Peachtree uses a "post" icon, QuickBooks has an "OK" button on all transactions screens, and One-Write Plus uses a "save" icon to initiate posting. If you try to exit from the transaction screen without posting or saving, you are reminded to do so or "abandon the transaction."

The debits and credits of this posting process were stated briefly in each of the preceding sections of this chapter. It may be helpful to summarize the postings for all sales/accounts receivable transactions for your review:

Sales on Account:
- cause a debit (increase) to accounts receivable
- and a credit (increase) to sales revenue

plus for Inventory Sales:
- cause a debit (increase) to cost of goods sold
- and a credit (decrease) to inventory

Sales for Cash:
- cause a debit (increase) to cash
- and a credit (increase) to sales revenue

plus for Inventory Sales:
- cause a debit (increase) to cost of goods sold
- and a credit (decrease) to inventory

Receipts on Account:
- cause a debit (increase) to cash
- and a credit (decrease) to accounts receivable

Returns/Adjustments:
- cause a debit (decrease) to sales returns and allowances
- and a credit (decrease) to accounts receivable

Don't worry! All of these things are taken care of for you automatically by the accounting software. All of these accounts are maintained as separate records in the general ledger, and the sales-related accounts are, of course, used to determine net income. The ending balance in the accounts receivable account in the general ledger will "match" (or balance to) the total of all the ending balances in the accounts receivable customer accounts.

But just in case you really want to know what your software is up to, Figure 7-8 provides an example of Peachtree's posting integration between accounts receivable and general ledger. The upper half of the figure displays a sales transaction in the sales journal that has already been posted to a customer account and to the general ledger sales account. The lower half of the figure shows the transaction as it would appear in the sales account within the general ledger. Please notice that this transaction increases both the customer account and the sales account.

Figure 7-8: *Sales transaction posted to general ledger account*

Bellweather Cleaning Services
Sales Journal

Date	Acco	Account Description	Invoice	Line Description	Debit Amnt	Credit Amnt
10/15	2350	Sales Tax Payable	9008	GA: State of GA Sales Tax		1.80
	2350	Sales Tax Payable		GWINNETT:		
				Gwinnett County Sales Tax		.68
	3225	Supplies Sales Revenue		Standard office waste basket; black plastic		45.00
	4000	Cost of Goods Sold		Cost of Sales	25.61	
	1320	Product Inventory		Cost of Sales		25.61
	1200	Accounts Receivable		Andy's Sporting Goods	47.48	
			Total		73.09	73.09

Bellweather Cleaning Services
General Ledger

Account ID	Date	Jnl	Trans Description	Debit Amt	Credit Amt	Balance
Account Description	Refer					
3225	10/1		Beginning Balance			-2,169.48
Supplies Sales Revenue						
	10/15 9008	SJ	Andy's Sporting Goods -Item: BWST-3QPL-Standard office waste basket; black plastic		45.00	
	10/18 9012	SJ	Hines Bicycle Repair - Item: C1500-105FL - 1 quart liquid floor wax for vinyl floor.	125.00		
			Current Period Change	170.00		-170.00
	10/31		**Ending Balance**			**-2,339.48**

Applying Finance Charges

Finance charges are the interest you apply against a customer balance if the amount is not paid within the agreed upon time frame. For example, if the selling terms are "Net 30," with 1.5 percent per month late charges applied after thirty days, the accounting software is usually designed to recognize which accounts are unpaid after the thirty day limit and automatically calculate and apply the late fee (finance charge). Most low-end accounting packages require you to execute a command that triggers the process of calculating and applying finance charges, so you can be in control of who gets charged and when it happens. You must be careful to put this on your "to do" list.

In QuickBooks, for example, you establish a finance charge rate as a master record item; that rate is then applied to each customer that you check off ☑ when you decide to assess the charges. Figure 7-9 gives you a peek at the method of assessing finance charges. You can select the "mark all" button on the right to have QuickBooks apply the charge to all customers with invoices that are overdue, *or* you can check off each customer individually, *or* you can mark all, then uncheck any customers that you want to excuse from the finance charge. Once you view and mark the list, clicking on "OK" causes the amount in the "fin charge" column to be added to the customer balance due. These charges will appear on the next invoice you send to that customer or on month-end statements (see the next chapter for more on customer statements).

Figure 7-9: *Procedure to assess finance charges*

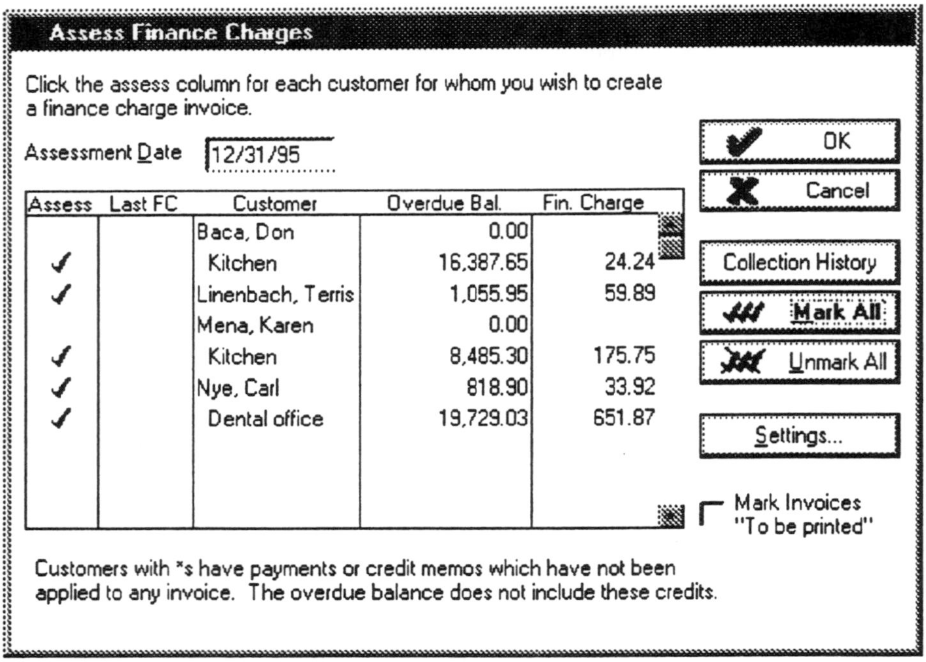

The action of applying finance charges causes a debit (increase) to accounts receivable and a credit (increase) to some form of revenue account (often "miscellaneous income"). This debit and credit are displayed either in a special journal report (like a finance charge journal), or as a transaction entry in the sales journal.

Saving and Backing Up Your Data

No modern accounting package is worth its price unless it saves data to disk as you enter transactions—this happens in the post or save routine just discussed. Make backup copies of data files every day! Put it on your to-do list—use the backup procedure that is built into the software, and do it religiously! Most packages will provide a menu item for this procedure; if not, look to your computer's user's manual for advice. The procedure and an illustration of the backup process was contained in Chapter 2 "Choosing and Using Accounting Software."

Chapter Eight

Accounts Receivable Reports

Importance of Accounts Receivable Reports

Usually the most important area of management control for any business is the control of sales and collections. Information for decision making in this area comes from your accounts receivable (AR) module. Any computerized AR module will produce numerous reports; some of these are mandatory for managing your customer relations and satisfying financial analysis needs, others are optional for receivables management, and some are peculiar to various types of business but unnecessary to others. The discussions and illustrations in this chapter seek to introduce you to a variety of the AR reports that are available to you so that you can choose which ones will be most relevant to your business.

All accounting software provides you with the ability to customize existing reports in a way that suits you. This means that you can delete rows or columns, add rows or columns, specify your headings, or request various levels of subtotals. For example, the printed customer master file list can contain as little as the customer name, contact name, and phone number; or as much as all the data in the master file plus the customer balance, the date of the last transaction, and the date that the customer was placed in the file! Just five years ago, this customizing power was only available in software costing at least $5,000.

So let's get started on the path to your successful and satisfying use of accounts receivable reports so that you can collect the money owed to you—on time and with little hassle on your part.

Getting the Printed Results

Most accounting software packages will have a "reports" icon and/or main menu item labeled "reports," with "general ledger, accounts payable, accounts receivable, and payroll" as report categories within that menu. QuickBooks places the printing of lists and forms under the "file, print" menu in addition to having the traditional "reports" menu. One-Write Plus has a "print" selection under the "entries" menu, which leads to the printing of checks, invoices, statements, labels, etc. When you select "accounts receivable" reports or "customer" reports, you will be faced with many report choices. Here are the most common ones:

- aged receivables report
- cash receipts journal
- customer ledger reports
- customer mailing labels
- customer master list
- customer statements
- finance charge report
- sales activity analysis
- sales invoices
- sales journal (invoice register)
- sales tax reports

Make your choice from the reports list, and you will be prompted to specify some customizing choices like the period of time to include and some "filtering criteria." The use of filtering criteria (like selecting only retail customers and excluding all other types of customers) gives you the power to design finely tuned reports that better fit your needs. You should also be able to specify whether you want the reports displayed on screen or printed immediately. Peachtree shows the reports on screen (this is a default setting that you can alter if you choose to), and from the displayed report, you can click on a "print" icon.

Some of these AR reports are absolutely necessary to the functioning of your business, and some you will have to try out to determine if they are helpful. Let's take a look at the most important of these reports.

Absolutely Necessary Reports

The printed results of processing accomplished by your computer is called the audit trail (explained in detail in Chapter 3). The AR audit trail includes documents like the sales invoices you send to your customers; but, more importantly, it is comprised of the reports that give evidence of what transactions were recorded in the sales and accounts receivable accounts. For example, when checks are received and deposited, the cash receipts journal provides the "trail" that can be used to trace each receipt of money directly to a customer account, to a specific sales transaction, and even to the original invoice.

At the very least, the AR audit trail should include a sales journal, cash receipts journal, and customer ledger. Some accountants would also argue that sales tax reports and the aged receivables report should be included in the minimum audit trail. Many other reports are usually available at a keystroke; I will try to describe enough of them within this chapter to help you decide what you need for your situation.

Necessary for Your Customers

Sales Invoices

The presentation of accurate and timely sales invoices is normally the key to collecting what is owed to you. Your sales invoice is the official document addressed to a customer, detailing the items or services sold, and requesting payment by a specific date. The invoice date becomes important for calculating the discount date (if appropriate) and the due date. The discount date is the deadline for a customer to subtract a discount from the amount due, and the due date is the date which has been agreed upon as the date by which the payment must be made to avoid finance charges (if used). Figure 8-1 provides an example of a customer invoice produced by QuickBooks.

Your AR software will probably provide you with the option of printing invoices as you enter the data for each sale, or to print them in a group at the end of a day or week. In Figure 7-5 (the sales/invoicing screen), you can see an icon labeled "print" with a small printer on it—click this, and the invoice will print as soon as you fill in the appropriate data. If you click the "post" or "OK" icon, the invoice will be posted and saved for you to print later. In either case, the software will let you print or display a listing (invoice register) of printed and/or unprinted invoices so you can keep your place in the process.

Figure 8-1: *Sample sales invoice*

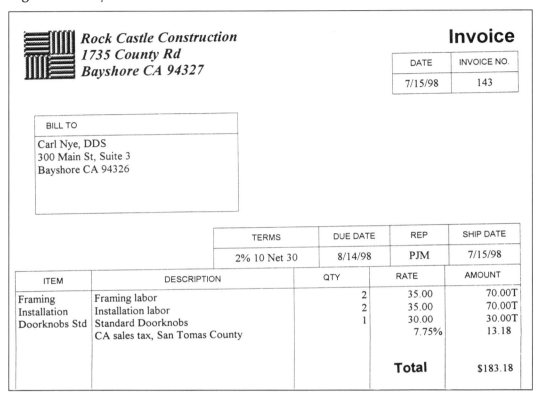

					Invoice	
Rock Castle Construction				DATE	INVOICE NO.	
1735 County Rd				7/15/98	143	
Bayshore CA 94327						

BILL TO

Carl Nye, DDS
300 Main St, Suite 3
Bayshore CA 94326

TERMS	DUE DATE	REP	SHIP DATE
2% 10 Net 30	8/14/98	PJM	7/15/98

ITEM	DESCRIPTION	QTY	RATE	AMOUNT
Framing	Framing labor	2	35.00	70.00T
Installation	Installation labor	2	35.00	70.00T
Doorknobs Std	Standard Doorknobs	1	30.00	30.00T
	CA sales tax, San Tomas County		7.75%	13.18
	Total			$183.18

An interesting option of the invoice printing process is the "style" of the finished product. The sample in Figure 8-1 would be called a "plain paper, graphic enhanced style." In the AR defaults or the printing default settings, you should be able to specify which size and style of invoice you want to use. For example, you can choose 8.5" x 11" plain paper invoices, 8.5" x 11" graphic invoices (even with your company logo), 8.5" x 5.5" half page size, or 8.5" x 11" data-only invoices, which print on forms that you purchase from an office supply source. Peachtree and QuickBooks even allow you to design your own invoice layout by changing where the data fields will appear on the form, or adding your own wording.

Customer Statements

The customer statement is a period end listing of the activity for one customer, with the ending balance due emphasized. Some businesses mail statements at the end of the month instead of mailing individual invoices; some businesses forgo statements because they mail individual invoices. Very few companies would mail both of these.

Figure 8-2 from Peachtree gives you a general idea of a customer statement's contents: the customer name and address, the statement date, the invoicing date, due date, invoice number or receipt number (reference), description, amount of each transaction for that specific customer, and a running balance. If a finance charge has been assessed, this will show on the statement. The ending running balance is repeated at the bottom of the statement as the total due. Some software also breaks down the amount due into aging periods (current, more than thirty days, more than sixty days, etc.) as seen in this figure.

Figure 8-2: *Sample customer statement*

Bellweather Cleaning Services
1505 Pavilion Place. Suite C
Norcross, GA 30092

Statement
Statement Date: Mar 15, 1995
Customer Account ID: HZ-100-9

Voice: 564-5700
Fax: 564-5888

Account Of: Hines Bicycle Repair
Box 1499
Atlanta, GA 30303
USA

Amount Enclosed
$_____

Date	Date Due	Reference	Paid	Description	Amount	Balance
11/9/94	12/9/94	1908		Verbal	639.60	639.60
12/15/94	1/14/95	1911	Part	Verbal–Jim	84.00	723.60
1/6/95	2/1/95	1924		Verbal	213.33	936.93
3/3/95	4/1/95	1035		5009-10	170.34	1,107.27
3/14/95	4/13/95	1041		HBR20-100	462.43	1,569.70

					Total	1,569.70

0 – 30	31 – 60	61 – 90	Over 90 days
632.77	297.33		639.60

Most AR software will allow you to specify the starting and ending date, starting and ending customer to print, whether to print zero and credit balance statements, the minimum balance necessary to print that statement, and whether to print statements for accounts with no activity for the period. You do not need to retain a copy of each statement that you mail since all the activity on a statement can be easily viewed on demand and is printed as the customer ledger detail report. (And you are keeping backup copies of your data, right?)

Necessary for Operational Control

Customer Ledger Reports

The purpose of the customer ledger report is to list the current status of each customer and all of the detailed activity for each customer during the current period. This report would be alphabetized by customer name and would list for each customer the previous period balance owed, the details of all current transactions, and the ending balance owed on a specific date. This report is used as the reference tool for answering customer inquiries, settling disputes about account balances, and surveying the recent history of specific customers.

As you can see from the QuickBooks customer ledger report shown in Figure 8-3, there are columns for customer name, transaction type, date, transaction reference, transaction amount as a debit or credit, and the running balance. The debits to these accounts are usually the sales you have made, and the credits are usually the payments you have received from that customer.

Figure 8-3: *Customer ledger—detailed listing*

Rock Castle Construction
Customer Balance Detail
As of December 31, 1995

Type	Date	Num	Debit	Credit	Balance
Mena, Karen					0.00
Kitchen					0.00
Invoice	9/29/95	133	10,815.38		10,815.38
Invoice	10/20/95	134	17,699.92		28,485.30
Payment	11/1/95			5,000.00	23,485.30
Payment	11/15/95			5,000.00	18,485.30
Payment	12/1/95			10,000.00	8,485.30
Total Kitchen			28,485.30	20,000.00	8,485.30
Total Mena, Karen			28,485.30	20,000.00	8,485.30
Nye, Carl					0.00
Dental Office					0.00
Invoice	9/11/95	131	10,213.20		10,213.20
Invoice	9/25/95	132	19,729.03		29,942.23
Payment	10/8/95			10,213.20	19,729.03
Payment	10/23/95			19,729.03	0.00
Total Dentist Office			29,942.23	29,942.23	0.00
Total Nye, Carl			29,942.23	29,942.23	0.00

(this is a partial report)

Please note that this report does not include the general ledger account numbers used in the transaction; any transaction in the customer ledger can be traced to the journals by use of the journal reference (e.g., "invoice" or "payment"). The customer ledger report should always include a grand total at the bottom of the report (not shown in this figure) so that this amount can be compared with the ending balance in the accounts receivable account in the general ledger for the same date. Ensuring that these two figures are in balance is called "reconciling accounts receivable" and is considered a good internal control procedure.

The customer ledger report above is a detailed report. You could also print the customer ledger in summary form with just the customer name and the ending balance at a specific date. In traditional accounting terminology, this is called the schedule of accounts receivable and is not often used when you print the detailed version.

Sales Journal (for Credit Sales)

The Sales Journal is your written record of transactions that have increased the balances in your customer ledger accounts. It should be arranged in date order and includes the sales invoice number, the customer name, the accounts and amounts being debited, the accounts and amounts being credited, and a total of all sales to all customers for the specified period of time. A description of the transaction might also be included. An example from Peachtree is shown in Figure 8-4.

An examination of the first transaction in this figure reveals the major purpose of this journal. This transaction shows a credit (increase) to services revenue, account 3000, and a debit (increase) to accounts receivable, account 1200. The second transaction is more complex because it involves the sale of inventory and the collection of sales taxes. Follow along with Figure 8-4 here:

- "Sales Tax Payable," account 2350, is credited (increased) for three different tax authorities
- "Other Services Revenue," account 3200, is credited (increased)
- "Supplies Provided Revenue," account 3225, is credited (increased)
- "Cost of Goods Sold," account 4000, is debited (increased) to record the cost ($20.68) of the $31.25 supplies that were provided on this job
- "Cleaning Supplies Inventory," account 1300, is credited (decreased) to remove this cost from inventory
- the gross amount of the sale plus sales taxes is debited (increased) to accounts receivable, account 1200—Fred's Pet Salon

This shows how the transaction is distributed into accounts in the General Ledger and Customer Ledger.

Figure 8-4: *Sample sales journal*

Date	Account ID	Account Description	Invoice	Customer	Debit Amnt	Credit Amnt
		Bellweather Cleaning Services				
		Sales Journal				
		For the Period From Mar 1, 1995 to Mar 31, 1995				
3/1/95	3000	Commercial Services Revenues	1031	Sampson High School		400.00
	1200	Accounts Receivable			400.00	
3/1/95	2350	Sales Tax Payable	1032	Fred's Pet Salon		16.25
	2350	Sales Tax Payable				4.06
	2350	Sales Tax Payable				4.07
	3200	Other Services Revenues				375.00
	3225	Supplies Provided				31.25
	4000	Cost of Goods Sold			20.68	
	1300	Cleaning Supplies Inventory				20.68
	1200	Accounts Receivable			430.63	
3/2/95	2350	Sales Tax Payable	1034	Corporate Computer Sales		7.87
	2350	Sales Tax Payable				1.97
	2350	Sales Tax Payable				1.96
	3225	Supplies Provided				73.70
	4000	Cost of Goods Sold			95.64	
	1320	Product Inventory				95.64
	3225	Supplies Provided				123.00
	4000	Cost of Goods Sold			174.82	
	1320	Product Inventory				174.82
	3350	Shipping Charges Reimbursed				9.75
	1200	Accounts Receivable			218.25	
3/2/95	2350	Sales Tax Payable	1033	Moore Accounting Services		22.00
	2350	Sales Tax Payable				5.50
	2350	Sales Tax Payable				5.50
	3000	Commercial Services Revenues				175.00

(this is a partial report)

The Sales Journal is sometimes referred to as an Invoice Register, although some packages print an Invoice Register in addition to a Sales Journal. The Invoice Register usually only lists invoice totals by invoice number and date—and does not detail sales taxes or the various sales accounts to be charged. A company does not need both of these reports; I recommend the Sales Journal as a better audit trail.

Cash Receipts Journal

The purpose of the cash receipts journal is to provide the details of each receipt of cash or check whether it be from customers on account, from cash sales, or from the interest on your bank account. This journal is also printed in date order and contains most of the same columns as the sales journal. Figure 8-5 provides a sample Cash Receipt Journal from One-Write Plus. Because this journal contains all intake of cash, each transaction will have a debit (increase) to cash (in this case account 1098). Take special note of the account names and numbers that appear here—the purpose of this report is to show the distribution of the transaction to accounts in the general ledger and in the customer ledger. In this example, the first transaction credits (increases) sales account 4000 and debits (increases) cash account 1098. The other transactions increase cash and decrease accounts receivable.

Figure 8-5: *Sample cash receipts journal*

The Kite Store
CASH RECEIPT JOURNAL
1/1/96 To 2/28/96

DATE	TT	ID	NAME	SLS	REF NO	D	AMOUNT
1/20/96	CS	BREEZY	Breezy City Kites		00034298		654.87
		4000 - Sales			654.87 cr		
		1098 - Undeposited Cash			654.87 dr		
1/20/96	CR	KITEWORL	Kite World		00000765	D	7,258.84
		1100 - Accounts Receivable			7,258.84 cr		
		1098 - Undeposited Cash			7,258.84 dr		
2/21/96	CR	SUMMER	The Summer Shop		00000846		200.00
		1100 - Accounts Receivable			200.00 cr		
		1098 - Undeposited Cash			200.00 dr		
			TOTAL RECEIPTS				8,113.71

Other Useful Accounts Receivable Reports

Aged Receivables Report

The customer ledger, discussed above, provides the detail of activity for each customer; the aged receivables report provides that same customer data in summary form. The amounts owed by each customer are totaled by age categories—those amounts that are "current" (not yet due), those that are one to thirty days overdue, those that are thirty-one to sixty days overdue, those that are sixty-one to ninety days overdue, and those that are more than ninety days old. Figure 8-6 illustrates an aged receivables report from QuickBooks that is broken down by these categories.

With most modern accounting packages you can specify how to group your accounts. For example, you could use forty-five and ninety days as the only cutoffs.

Figure 8-6: *Aged receivables report*

Rock Castle Construction
A/R Aging Detail
As of December 15, 1995

Type	Date	Num	Name	Terms	Due Date	Aging	Open Balance
Current							
Invoice	11/28/95	137	Baca, Don: Kitchen	Net 30	12/28/95		16,387.65
Invoice	12/5/95	138	Reid Prop.: 75 suns...	Net 30	1/4/96		33,572.25
Invoice	12/10/95	144	Ahl, Fred: Family Room	Net 30	1/9/96		215.50
Total Current							50,175.40
1-30							
Invoice	10/20/95	134	Mena, Karen: Kitchen	Net 30	11/19/95	26	8,485.30
Total 1-30							8,485.30
31-60							
Invoice	9/25/95	132	Nye, Carl: Dental Office	Net 30	10/25/95	51	19,729.03
Invoice	10/10/95	133	Green, Hayley	Net 30	11/9/95	36	150.86
Total 31 - 60							19,879.88
61-90							
Invoice	9/8/95	142	Nye, Carl	Net 30	10/8/95	68	818.90
Total 61-90							818.90
>90							
Invoice	8/8/95	141	Linenbach, Terris	Net 30	9/7/95	99	1,055.95
Total>90							1,055.95
TOTAL							**80,415.43**

The subtotals on this report allow you to see at a glance the magnitude of each overdue category; you may then want to set a goal to reduce the over sixty day category by a desired percentage within a certain period of time. You can see that this report would also be used by management to zero in on those delinquent customers who are the most overdue on their payments. In fact, this report is usually used to trigger collection letters urging customers to pay up.

Customer Master List

A small business considers its customer list to be its gold mine and takes extremely good care of that list! The customer master list provides a list of all the data on file for each customer. This listing will present in tabular format all the fields you see when you create or maintain the customer records. Figure 8-7 provides an example from Peachtree. This listing normally includes such items as customer ID, customer name, address, contact name, various phone numbers, sales tax code, payment terms, default sales account numbers, and the current balance with this customer. Although Peachtree omits some of these items, other software packages include all of these and more. The customer master list is commonly used as a "contact initiator" where sales reps make phone calls to renew contact with customers and then write notations on a hard copy of the master list to be used in updating the file. Some businesses use this, along with a vendor master list, as sort of a quick reference phone book of their important business contacts. You could print this report every month, or it may be more practical to print it only a few times a year.

Figure 8-7: *Sample customer master list*

	Bellweather Cleaning Services Customer Master File List		
Customer ID **Customer**	**Address line 1** **Address line 2** **City ST ZIP**	**Contact** **Telephone 1** **Telephone 2** **Fax Number**	**Tax Code** **Resale No** **Terms** **Cust Since**
ASG100-94 Andy's Sporting Goods	Box 109 Duluth, GA 30093 USA	Andy Ardmore 404-564-1001 404-565-8100 404-564-8105	GWINNETT 2% 10, Net 30 Days 12/3/93
CC100-91 Corporate Computer Sales	PO Box 4519 Roswell, GA 30076 USA	Lynn Culpepper 404-587-1000 404-587-1202 404-587-2311	FULTON 2% 10, Net 30 Days 12/1/93
COL200-820 Cirus Office Leasing Group	190 Pleasant Hill Road Norcross, GA 30092 USA	Rocky Richards 404-564-4910 404-564-4810 404-564-1516	FULTON 2% 10, Net 30 Days 12/3/93
E010 Ernie's Dry Cleaning	1900 Gaslight Tower Atlanta, GA 30303 USA	Ernie Jackson 404-423-1000 404-423-1012 404-423-1001	FULTON 2% 10, Net 30 Days 8/10/94

(this is a partial report)

Customer Mailing Labels

I recommend that you use window envelopes for mailing invoices and statements because low-end accounting software does not usually print mailing labels in the order of, and only for, the invoices that you have just prepared (QuickBooks is the exception). Of course you might need mailing labels when you are sending a special sale announcement, discount offer, or your annual price list or catalog. Peachtree, QuickBooks, and One-Write Plus can print mailing labels in various order (by zip code for example) and for a type of customer (like retail or wholesale). Check the user's manual to see what options are available for size and style of labels.

Sales History Analysis Reports

Whether you sell a product or a service, you have probably always wanted to have a better handle on where your strengths and weaknesses are in the sales arena. Most accounting software provides you with some form of sales analysis reports. In Figure 8-8 from One-Write Plus, you can see that this type of report groups sales transactions by type of item sold for a specified period of time. Alternately, you can select a sales analysis by customer, by revenue account, or by salesperson. This report is useful for identifying sales trends by printing it each month and comparing month to month activity. You might also use it to identify seasonally heavy periods or the slack periods when sales and special offerings could be most effective.

Figure 8-8: *Sample sales activity report*

	The Kite Store **SALES ANALYSIS BY ITEM REPORT** 1/1/96 To 3/31/96			
ITEM ID	ITEM NAME	QTY ORD	QTY SHI	AMOUNT
BLUE	Blue Paper Kite	22	22	218.90
GLIDER	Lightweight Hang Glider	15	15	25,439.85
GREEN	Green Silk Kite	25	25	748.75
PINK	Pink Silk Kite	27	27	538.65
RED	Red Paper Kite	19	19	189.05
WHITE	White Paper Kite	16	16	143.20
YELLOW	Yellow Silk Kite	22	22	658.90
			TOTAL SALES:	27,937.30

Accounts Receivable Graphs

Peachtree offers a feature called the collection manager, and QuickBooks has a main menu devoted to "graphs" (One-Write Plus offers no graphs but data can be exported to a spreadsheet or word processing program to create graphics).

This part of the AR module provides you with the power to view your unpaid receivables as a bar chart grouped by age of the receivables and to drill down to any details behind the graph. Figure 8-9 shows a bar graph from Peachtree that depicts on a specific date and by age group, the amount of receivables (shown by the height of the bars). You can switch to a pie chart by clicking the "graph type" icon, and you can send the graph to paper by clicking on "printer." Management can use these graphs to compare collection results on a month to month basis.

Figure 8-9: *Sample receivables graph*

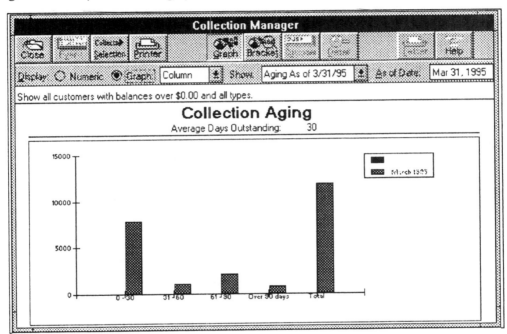

The "drill-down" feature applies here in that you can direct the mouse pointer to any bar on the graph and double-click to see the list of AR items that make up the data for that bar. Once you see the customer balances listed, you can drill down further by double-clicking on any transaction to see the original invoice or payment. In Peachtree, you can even drill down to a customer in one of the overdue categories and then click the "letter" icon to produce a collection letter.

Taxable Sales Report

A sales report that contains a column for "sales tax" may be required by the taxing authority in your state, city, or county. Even if it isn't required, you will be interested in knowing that the amount charged to sales taxes payable in your general ledger is absolutely correct. Why? Because you have to write a check to the government monthly or quarterly based on the taxes collected from your customers. Unless you have a detailed report of this, the taxing authority will require you to pay a percentage of total gross revenue, which may be too high if you have some tax-exempt sales. Figure 8-10 shows a sales tax report produced by QuickBooks. You may notice that this report includes only the total sales and the total sales tax collected in each tax category. If you need to know the sales tax collected on each sale, you could print the detailed contents of the sales tax payable account from the general ledger.

Figure 8-10: *Sales tax summary report*

Rock Castle Construction
Sales Tax Liability Report
October through December 1995

	Total Sales	Non-Tax...	Taxable Sales	Tax Rate	Tax	Sales Tax Paya... As of Dec 31, '95
State Board of Equalization						
San Domingo	86,576.50	1,960.00	84,616.50	7.50%	6,346.24	4,859.40
San Tomas	16,739.00	0.00	16,739.00	7.75%	1,297.27	161.20
State Board of Equalization - ...	0.00	0.00	0.00	0.00	0.00	0.00
Total State Board of Equalization						5,020.60
TOTAL						**5,020.60**

What to Save/What to Ignore

Your accounts receivable software will probably produce more reports than you will ever need. When you first start working with an AR system, it is a good idea to experiment with all the various reports that each module provides. You will need to match the information provided on the reports with your needs and personal preferences. Try to keep in mind that your business history is represented by your accounting reports, and choose among the available reports with "comparability" in mind. In other words, print reports on a periodic basis that can be compared to previous periods for reasonableness, growth, and general business health. Experience will tell you what is necessary and what is excess.

My recommendation for the minimum set of AR reports to be printed and filed for each period in a book or folder is:

- detailed customer ledger listing
- sales journal

- cash receipts journal
- taxable sales report

If you intend to compare sales activity from period to period, then a detailed sales activity report (possibly with an accompanying graph) should also be filed at specified intervals you choose.

If the collection of accounts in a timely manner is a problem for your business, you will really appreciate the aged receivables report. If the volume of your AR transactions and your customer list is small, you can probably skip the aged receivables report. Some businesses use the month-end statement approach; others send out invoices at the time of the sale and do not send statements at all. Analyze your needs and decide what is best for your business.

Exporting Accounts Receivable Reports to Other Software

Exporting reports or files from accounting software to other applications is a fairly advanced computer skill, but you may want to experiment with it. You will probably find many reasons why you would want to use some set of data from your AR system in another computer activity like special catalog mailings to customers, spreadsheet analysis of customer month end balances compared side by side for twelve months, or a report that lists high activity customers whom you have chosen to receive a Christmas gift. You will find other examples at the end of Chapters 4, 6, and 10. Figure 8-11 shows an example document using WordPerfect to write a report that includes a list of our best customers that has been exported from QuickBooks.

The process for accomplishing this task generally involves these four steps:

1. Display and/or print the report in AR that contains the data you want in your spreadsheet or word processor.
2. Select the "file, export" commands from the print or file menus.
3. Specify your preferences for exporting, such as which fields to export and what type of export file to create (e.g., a plain text file, a tab delimited data file, or a specific spreadsheet file), and where to store it (e.g., the A: drive, or a special subdirectory on C:).
4. Open your spreadsheet or word processor software and use the "file, import," "file, open," "file, retrieve," or "tools, import" command to open the file saved in the third step.

Figure 8-11: *WordPerfect document using accounts receivable data*

INTERNAL MEMORANDUM

TO: Rockcastle Construction Contract Reps
FROM: Jan Goodman, Sales Director
DATE: October 20, 1999
SUBJECT: **Giving Thanks!**

You will be pleased to learn that we have decided to offer our best customers a Thanksgiving gift in honor of our 10th Anniversary. We have pulled a list of our customers who have billed more than $1000 in sales thus far this year and want to offer them a $100 gift certificate sometime during Thanksgiving week to thank them for their business. John and I feel that it is most appropriate that each of you be able to inform each of your clients personally of this offer. We will prepare special 'certificates' for each of these customers and distribute them to you by November 10. Here are the lucky recipients:

Sales by Customer as of October 15

Baca, Don	16,387.65
Courtney, Ed	3,091.38
Green, Hayley	1,150.85
Gutmann, Jean	2,262.75
Linenbach, Terris	1,055.95
Mena, Karen	8,485.30
Carl Nye	20,731.11
Reid Properties	33,572.25

At this point, the list of items from your AR file can be manipulated within the word processing document. Refer to your user's manuals for the accounting, word processing, or spreadsheet programs to master importing and exporting files. Experiment—it's fun and rewarding!

Have you made a backup copy of your accounting files today?

Chapter Nine

Payroll

Introduction to Payroll

Everyone knows that the most important function of a payroll system is to produce accurate and timely paychecks—we've all been dependent on these at one time or another! Additionally, the company's payroll needs to comply with tax laws by calculating an appropriate amount of taxes associated with the payroll. Some of these taxes are deducted from the employee's paycheck (called withholding) and later paid to the government on the employee's behalf; other taxes are based on payroll and paid only by the employer. Payroll liability accounts (like medicare taxes payable and health insurance premiums payable) should be updated each pay period so that an accumulative amount owed to taxing and insurance institutions can be maintained. Periodically, you will have to file reports of your employee payroll activity, such as the quarterly IRS Form 941 that reports gross earnings and taxes withheld for each of your employees.

All of these activities can be accomplished using modern accounting software packages like One-Write Plus, QuickBooks, and Peachtree. Some packages offer more sophisticated and comprehensive capabilities than others, but you can write a payroll check with any of them. This chapter introduces you to these payroll functions and explains the computer work that goes on behind the data entry and menu choices.

Outside Payroll Services

If you have never handled the preparation of payroll before, you might want to consider an alternative to doing it "in-house." Many small businesses delegate this task to an outside agency that specializes in payroll preparation and therefore knows the payroll tax laws in detail. Some banks offer this service to commercial account holders because the payroll check amounts can be instantly deducted from the business account and can be electronically deposited to employee accounts at the same bank. This type of service is known as an "outside payroll service." Look in your telephone book for a local provider.

When a business uses an outside payroll service, they will receive periodic reports summarizing their payroll expenses and cash paid. These reports are then used to record a journal entry for payroll in the accounting system. The general journal of Chapter 2 is normally used for this purpose.

Payroll Accounting Concepts

The "Navigation Aid" from Peachtree for Windows provides a capsule view of any payroll system (see Figure 9-1). From this figure, you can see that employee records and a payroll transaction entry are the common sources of input data. The computer calculates net pay and taxes and produces paychecks and a payroll journal. The general ledger and employee records are updated with the amounts from the paychecks. The only thing missing from this picture is the important component of tax tables and the company master file, which directs the handling of taxes plus pension plans, health insurance, vacation time, sick days, and other employee benefits.

Figure 9-1: *Payroll navigation aid from Peachtree*

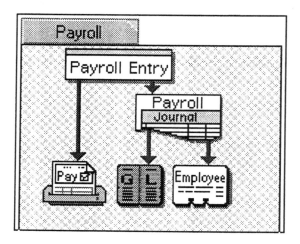

The detailed flowchart of Figure 9-2 describes a payroll system in more detail. As with previous applications described in this book, it is helpful to break down the parts of the system into the input, processing, and output steps that take place in payroll processing. Let's take a few moments to understand the overall picture of the mechanics of a payroll system.

Figure 9-2: *Payroll data flow*

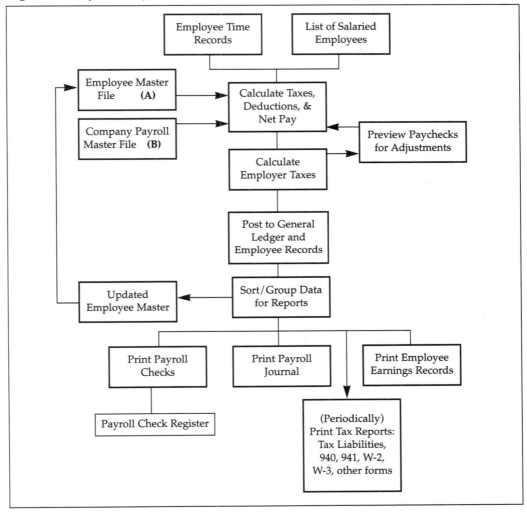

Input

The master files, marked (A) and (B) in Figure 9-2, take a lot of time and very careful attention to create because they specify how each employee should be paid. With these master files in place, all the other functions on this flowchart happen with lightening speed and will be accurate every time. The employee master file contains each employee's name, address, pay rate or salary, social security number, tax filing status, number of allowances, and optional choices for pension plans and special deductions. The company master file contains the current annual tax tables for federal, state, and local taxes, as well as data for all employees (or groups of employees) regarding other deductions like health insurance, 401K's, union dues, etc. This second master file may also need to contain codes and procedures for handling tips, commissions, employee loans, travel advances, etc. The only other input to payroll comes on the last day of the pay period when you enter hours worked or select which salaried employees are entitled to pay. This step kicks the weekly or periodic payroll process into gear.

Processing

When the paymaster enters hours worked for hourly employees, or selects the appropriate salaried employees, the computer calculates all deductions and net pay. All the software I have used lets you preview on-screen the resulting gross pay, deductions, and net pay. If you click "OK" on this preview, the computer will post (copy) payroll expenses, tax expenses, tax liabilities, and a cash reduction into the general ledger, and will print the paychecks. The employee master file will be updated with both current and year to date (YTD) salary data for each paycheck, and you can then choose from a variety of reports to print because the computer will sort and group the payroll data in any manner that is needed for management analysis.

Output

The most important printed output is the payroll check, which should be followed by a check register listing of those checks. A payroll journal (or payroll transaction register) that details all of the debits and credits to expense, asset, and liability accounts provides the audit trail for payroll. Although you may not need it every pay period, the YTD earnings record of every employee should be printed periodically as part of the accounting audit trail. Other reports are printed depending on what taxes and deductions you must pay. For example, any company who hires employees must comply with federal and state tax laws that require you to report all employee earnings and deductions on, at least, a quarterly basis using a form called the IRS 941 Form. Depending on the size of your payroll, you will have to make payments to various taxing bodies on a monthly or quarterly basis based on the taxes you withheld from employees; these payments are accompanied by other forms. In addition, you will need to produce W-2 and W-3 Forms at the end of the year.

Debits and Credits behind the Payroll

You will understand better how the computer updates your financial records during the preparation of a payroll if you understand the reality of debits and credits (increases and decreases) that result from those paychecks. Preparing the payroll causes two journal entries to be created—one for the employees' paychecks, and one for the employer's taxes and obligations associated with those paychecks. These entries usually appear in summary form for all employees but may be easier to understand if you think of the effects caused by just one employee paycheck.

Salary Expense, Employee Tax Liabilities, and Net Pay

When Mary Smith earns $500 for the week, we prepare a paycheck for $390 in net pay because we withheld $48 in federal income tax, $24 in state income tax, $31 in FICA tax (Social Security), and $7 in Medicare tax to pay on her behalf. The rate for these taxes change annually, so check on the rates for future years with the IRS and update your software.

The $500 gross pay should be recorded as a debit (increase) to the salary expense (or wages expense) account. The $48, $24, $31, and $7 for taxes should be recorded as credits (increases) in the appropriate tax liability accounts—federal income tax payable, state income tax payable, FICA tax payable, and Medicare tax payable. These amounts are recorded in payable accounts because we will later pay those amounts to the government taxing agencies in Mary Smith's name. The $390 in net pay should be a credited to cash (or checking account) because this paycheck decreases cash. In journal entry form, this transaction would look like this:

		Debit	Credit
Jan 15	Salary Expense	$ 500	
	Federal Income Tax Payable		$48
	State Income Tax Payable		24
	FICA Tax Payable		31
	Medicare Tax Payable		7
	Cash (checking account)		390

In other words, the gross pay is charged to a payroll expense account, the taxes are charged to liability accounts, and the net pay is deducted from cash. If there are also deductions for health insurance or a pension plan, these amounts are recorded as liabilities (health premiums payable and pension contributions payable) and are later paid to the medical insurance company and the pension plan provider.

Employer Payroll Taxes and Tax Liabilities

Your company, as an employer, must pay an equal share of FICA tax and Medicare tax to match the employee amount. In addition, most employers must pay a percentage of gross wage for both federal and state unemployment insurance programs, and sometimes for state disability programs. These unemployment and disability taxes are usually paid only by the employer (not deducted from employee wages) and are incurred, and should be recorded, at the time a paycheck is written. As an example, using the federal rate of .8 percent (that's 8/10 of 1 percent) and an example state rate of 5.4 percent, the company must record $4 in federal unemployment taxes and $27 in state unemployment taxes on Mary Smith's $500 gross pay. Consequently, the employer payroll tax transaction should also record as credits (increases) $4 in federal unemployment tax payable and $27 in state unemployment tax payable. The total of these taxes is recorded as a debit (increase) in payroll tax expense. In journal form, the transaction would look like this:

		Debit	Credit
Jan 15	Payroll Tax Expense	$69	
	FICA tax payable		$31
	Medicare tax payable		7
	Federal unemployment tax payable		4
	State unemployment tax payable		27

If the employer also contributes to a pension plan, disability insurance, and/or pays the employee health insurance premiums, an entry would be made at the time of the payroll to debit (increase) employee benefits expense and credit (increase) health premiums payable, disability insurance payable, and/or pension contributions payable. Many other deductions from and additions to the gross pay might be necessary, and most modern accounting software can handle a variety of payroll scenarios ranging from wage garnishments to tip reporting.

All of this debiting and crediting is done automatically by the accounting software once you review the paycheck data and ask the system to produce a paycheck!

Setting up Company Defaults

In general, it takes a fair amount of time to set up a payroll system, but comparatively very little time to produce your payroll. A payroll system relies on certain default settings such as federal and state tax tables, federal and state unemployment tax rates, methods of deductions for annuity plans, group insurance, union dues, and other deductions. These settings are called the company defaults for payroll and are stored in a "company payroll master file"; QuickBooks calls them the "payroll items list." You can get an idea of the magnitude of items that must be set up as company defaults by browsing through the "payroll items list" for a sample company from QuickBooks in Figure 9-3. You can see from this list that federal and state taxes are just two of the items that might be deducted from an employee's wages. Accounting software must be capable of handling a variety of other additions and deductions like:

- local income and commerce taxes
- pension plan deductions
- state disability insurance taxes
- health insurance deductions
- union dues payable
- inclusion of commissions, tips, and/or employee loans
- handling of travel advances
- wage garnishments
- a variety of employee classes (hourly, salaried, commissioned, special)
- federal and state unemployment tax rates

Figure 9-3: *Payroll default items list*

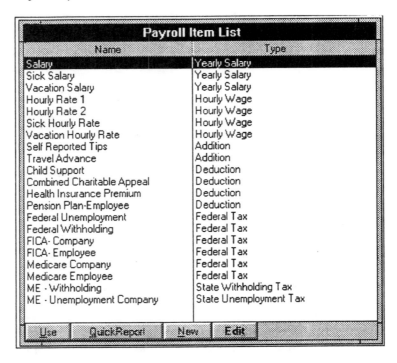

These defaults, e.g., the "payroll items list," must be set up by the user before an accurate set of paychecks can be produced. In addition, an "employee master file" (explained in the next section) contains the pay rates of individuals along with their tax filing status and other default settings that will cause automatic deductions at pay time. Once these default settings are specified, they are used over and over again to prepare each paycheck and rarely need to be changed.

Payroll Tax Tables

Federal income tax, FICA, Medicare, and state income tax tables that are used to calculate withholding taxes for each employee are supplied by the software vendor if your accounting package contains a payroll module. These tables rarely have to be modified within a calendar year, so most packages keep the tables "hidden"—you don't have to see them. In QuickBooks, you can't even view the tax tables, but Peachtree provides you with a "maintain company payroll tax tables" screen that allows you to specify the formula for any deductions you might need to apply to your payroll.

For example, you will normally need to specify your own state and federal unemployment tax rate. Check the "formula" area of this Peachtree screen in Figure 9-4 and you will see that the state unemployment tax is calculated at 5.4 percent of gross pay on adjusted gross income up to a maximum of $7,000. If your State unemployment tax rate was reduced because your company has few unemployment claims, you would use this screen to change the tax rate for all future payrolls.

Figure 9-4: *Sample payroll tax table edit capability*

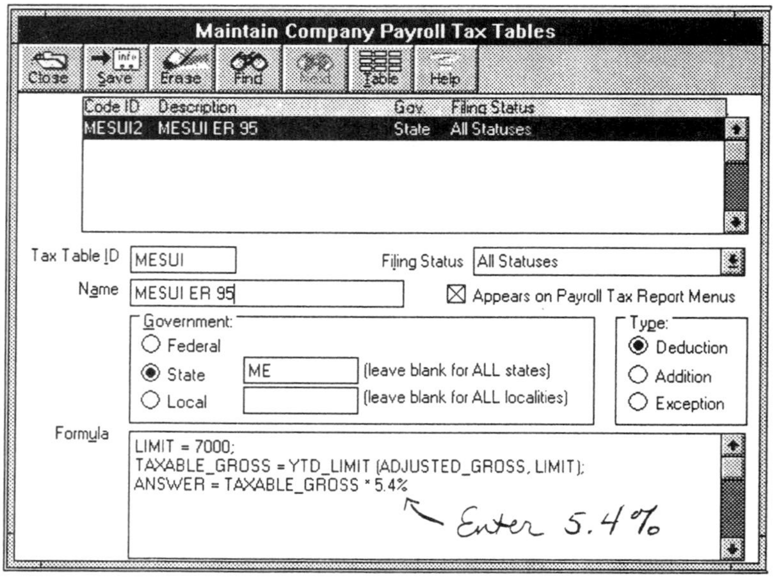

Tax Table Updates

All accounting software providers (Peachtree, Intuit, etc.) offer a payroll tax update service, whereby they will notify you when new federal and state tax tables become available; usually around mid-December of each year. You will pay a fee and receive a diskette with the appropriate new tax tables that can simply be copied over the old tax tables, using a computer routine that is specified with the diskette.

Pension Plans

There are a wide variety of options that companies are employing to provide their employees with opportunities for retirement planning. If you pay all the contributions for an employee pension plan, you can simply set this up as a calculation within the company-paid defaults. The amount might be a fixed amount per month or could be calculated as a percentage of gross pay. You would specify that this amount be calculated and recorded at the same time as the company payroll tax liability. Figure 9-5 provides you with an example of the set up screen used in One-Write Plus to specify that a 401K pension plan contribution will be recorded each pay period for each employee as a percentage of gross pay, to be placed on the employee card. An important factor to keep in mind about pension plans is that the pension plan contribution is sheltered from taxes. On the lower half of Figure 9-5, the default settings indicate that the deduction for this pension plan amount will be taken from gross pay before any taxes are calculated.

Figure 9-5: *Sample setup screen for pension plan*

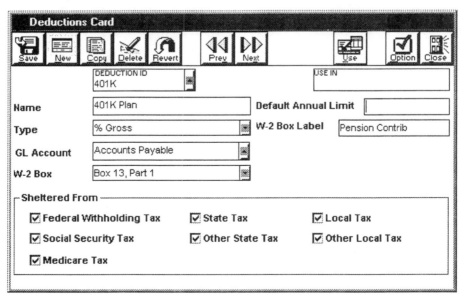

The employee contribution for a pension plan is specified as a "deduction field" in the employee master file for the amount to be withheld from the employee. Take a look at Figure 9-7 now, and you will see that on the employee master record, the "payroll info" tab on that screen is used to specify the rate of the pension plan deduction for a specific employee.

Medical Insurance

Another very common type of payroll benefit is a health insurance plan paid for by the employer and/or employee. Sometimes the health insurance premium for the employee is paid by the employer, with an option that the employee may join and pay for a group plan for other members of his/her family. Sometimes the full health insurance premium is paid by the employee (including any optional additional coverage for the family). Health insurance premiums paid by the employer are handled in a similar fashion to that just described above for pension plans—the deduction field for health insurance and the amount or a percentage are specified in the company defaults. Look for "health insurance premium" on the payroll items list of Figure 9-3. Health insurance premiums paid by the employee must be specified on the employee master record (look for "health insurance" on Figure 9-7).

Other Deductions

Your city or state probably has some equivalent of a "United Way" or "combined charitable appeals" fund raising campaign. If you deduct this type of contribution from your employee paychecks, then you can set up a field for this in the company payroll master file and specify the amount for each employee in the employee master file. A similar procedure would be used for union dues, savings plans, and wage garnishments (such as child support payments); a field can be set up for each of these in the company master file, with the amount then specified in the employee master record.

Federal and State Unemployment and Disability Taxes

Unemployment taxes, workers compensation insurance, and disability taxes are not deducted from the employee's wages but are usually paid solely by the employer. Some states do require an employee contribution, which would be handled like the FICA tax explained above. Unemployment benefits are provided under a joint federal and state program with the FUTA (Federal Unemployment Tax Act) rate of approximately 6.2 percent on the first $7,000 of wages and the SUTA (State Unemployment Tax Act) rate at 5.4 percent or less, depending on the actual rate of unemployment claims for a specific business. The federal government allows a credit against the FUTA rate of up to 5.4 percent for amounts contributed to SUTA. In this manner, a total tax of 6.2 percent can be levied with .8 percent going to FUTA and 5.4 percent going to SUTA. State Disability Insurance (SDI) tax rates and workers compensation insurance rates are also levied by individual states. All of these tax rates must be specified in the company payroll master file. (Check for current rates as you set up your accounting defaults.)

Figure 9-6 provides an example from the QuickBooks payroll setup screen where the federal unemployment tax defaults are entered or edited. For each payroll tax, you should specify the "expense account" to charge for the tax—notice that I have assigned it to "payroll expenses" in Figure 9-6 and that the tax amount will be credited to "payroll liabilities"—it is accumulated in this account and paid quarterly (see discussion later in this chapter).

Figure 9-6: *Unemployment tax rate setup*

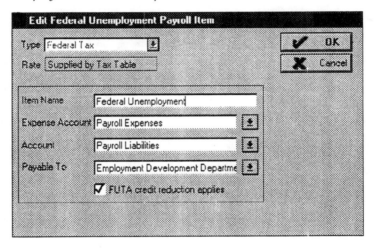

Setting Up the Employee Master File

Once all the company payroll defaults are complete, you must then set up a master record for each employee—the employee master file. Items that are typically found in an employee master file include:

- employee name and home address
- social security number
- telephone numbers
- pay rate or salary
- income tax filing status
- employee type (hourly, salaried, administration, operations)

- account numbers where wages and deductions will be charged
- deduction rate or amount for special items (pension, health insurance, etc.)
- hire date, review date, and other personnel data as needed

Figure 9-7: *Sample employee master file*

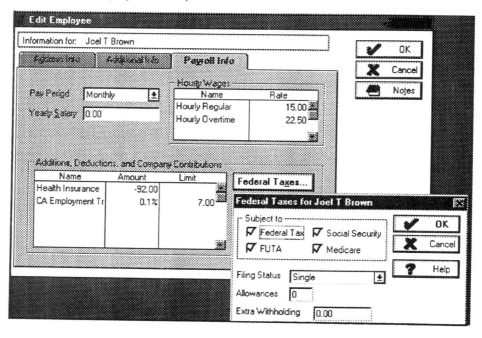

Figure 9-7 provides you with a look at the data entry screen for a new employee in QuickBooks. Page one and two, the "address info" and "additional info" tabs of this record (not shown in the figure), requires you to enter basic information like name, ID number, address, social security number, employee type, tax filing status, and hire date. The "payroll info" tab shown in Figure 9-7, provides space for you to enter hourly pay rates, or a yearly salary amount that is divided into weekly, biweekly, or monthly amounts on the paychecks. The "additions, deductions" section of this form is used to specify deductions like pension or health insurance contributions for this employee. When the "federal taxes" or "state taxes" button is clicked, it opens up a window where you can indicate the tax filing status and number of allowances the employee claims, as you can see in the bottom right corner of Figure 9-7. All accounting software packages offer a similar master record to record all the data for each employee.

Beginning Balances—Quarter to Date (QTD) and Year to Date (YTD)

The employee master file will eventually hold all the data for the earnings record of each employee. If you decide to begin using your new automated payroll system at some time other than the beginning of a new calendar year, then the accumulated earnings of your employees at the time of your start date must be entered into the employee record. One-Write Plus includes a "beginning balances" item on its "setup" menu for employee history. Figure 9-8 provides an example of the layout and type of data that is needed for each employee. Once you enter a pay date and employee name, click the "detail" icon to enter the specifics of a normal paycheck. After reviewing the data, and entering any changes, you would "save" that pay date and enter the next pay date for that employee until all year-to-date (YTD) data has been entered.

Figure 9-8: *Sample form for entering YTD earnings*

Date	Name	Hours	Gross Payroll	Tot W/H	Tot Ded	Ref No	X	Net Amount
1/15/96	Timothy A. Diehl	40.00	$480.00	$118.85	$19.00	TOTALS		$342.15
1/31/96	Timothy A. Diehl	34.00	$408.00	$104.82	$19.00	TOTALS		$284.18
2/15/96	Timothy A. Diehl	40.00	$480.00	$118.85	$19.00	TOTALS		$342.15
2/29/96	Timothy A. Diehl	20.00	$240.00	$59.05	$19.00	TOTALS		$161.95

DATE	TO THE ORDER OF		DESCRIPTION	REF NO	AMOUNT
2/29/96	Diehl, Timothy A.			TOTALS	$0.00

This historical data should be entered for each employee before the first paycheck is drawn because, remember, the tax calculation needs to know the accumulative gross pay to determine if it falls within the $62,700 FICA limit or the $7,000 unemployment tax limit. QuickBooks provides an entry screen for QTD and YTD earnings under the "payroll" item of the "activities" menu and allows you to enter these beginning balances as you find the time, even after your first paychecks are written, as long as the dates of the beginning balances and the gross pay ceilings are carefully adhered to. Peachtree includes a "beginning balances" button on the "maintain employees" screen.

Importance of Accumulative Earnings Balances

The federal and state governments are very interested in knowing how much you have paid each of your employees and how much you have withheld from their earnings in order to pay it into the government coffers. At the very least, you will be required to file a Form 941 (Employer's Quarterly Federal Tax Return) to the federal government and to any state government that levies income taxes. Some accounting software, like Peachtree, produces a Form 941 as a standard report. With the QTD and YTD earnings reports available in QuickBooks or One-Write Plus (and covered in the next chapter), you can easily fill in a Form 941. Your accumulative earnings records will be used to file other various reports to government agencies—and don't forget the W-2s that must be prepared at the end of a year (also covered in the next chapter).

Choosing the Conversion Date

The perfect time to convert your payroll function is at the beginning of a calendar year, but if that is not practical, don't wait! If you begin the use of a new payroll software system on January 1, you will not have to enter any accumulative QTD or YTD balances. If you choose not to do the conversion on January 1, however, it is best to start with your new software on April 1, July 1, or October 1 so you can enter the previous months' accumulative earnings data as YTD balances and not have to enter QTD balances. In other words, if you start using payroll on July 1, then the June 30 earnings balances are the YTD amount, and on July 1 the QTD balances would be zero. All payroll systems zero out the QTD accumulative totals at the end of each quarter in order to start a new quarter, so the QTD balances would start at zero on July 1. If you really must convert to your new payroll system in the middle of a quarter, then you will have to enter both QTD and YTD balances.

Producing Payroll Checks

Finally! After all that set up work, you get to see what a breeze it is to actually issue paychecks! Some accounting packages use an entry screen that looks like a time card, some use a form that looks like a check, and some use a list of employees where you check off the ones you need to pay. You might have ten employees. Peachtree, One-Write Plus, and QuickBooks let you designate which seven of them are paid weekly, and that the other three are paid at the end of each month. Peachtree also lets you go directly to a specific employee by selecting "payroll entry" from the "activities" menu. Once you specify an employee to pay, the software will present a screen where you can preview each paycheck. Figure 9-9 is an example from One-Write Plus.

Figure 9-9: *Sample payroll entry screen*

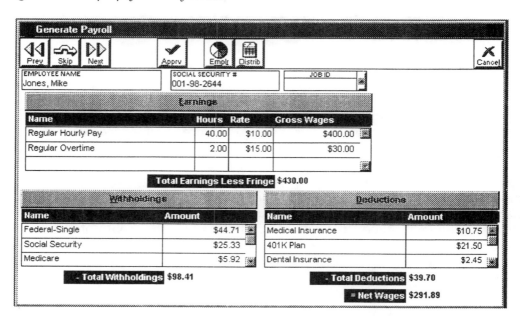

For the payroll entry in Figure 9-9, the software assumes that the person worked a regular forty hour week and calculates gross pay, deductions, and net pay using the hourly rate in the employee master file. You can change the hours in the "hours" field when an employee works less than forty hours, and you can type in hours for overtime when necessary. You may also overtype any amounts in the "withholdings" or "deductions" fields, and can even add deductions or earnings items. For example, you may need to deduct uniform costs on a one-time basis or add a bonus under earnings. The net wages on the paycheck are automatically recalculated as you make your changes.

Ready for a paycheck? Just click on the "approve" icon at the top of the screen and the paycheck information will be sent to the printer, while all the appropriate amounts are posted (copied) to general ledger accounts and to the employee master records. A sample paycheck with pay stub is shown in Chapter 10.

Payroll Check Register

Once all the checks have been printed for a pay period, a check register that lists these payroll checks should be printed. This register simply lists the date and check numbers, with payee (employees) and net pay amounts. The official audit trail for transactions that are activated by this payroll entry are detailed in a report called the payroll journal. (These reports are covered in Chapter 10).

Payroll Tax Liability Accounts

As you pay the payroll each period, a set of tax liability accounts is being built up in your general ledger. For example, remember that the paycheck entry will cause a credit (increase) in the FICA tax payable account, and the payroll tax expense entry will cause a credit (increase) in the FICA tax payable account for a matching amount. In other words, the FICA tax payable account will be accumulating a credit balance over the quarter. At the end of the quarter or month, you will be required to pay the accumulated balance of FICA, Medicare, unemployment, and income taxes withheld to an account at a local bank on behalf of the federal and state governments, usually accompanied by a Form 941. QuickBooks makes it especially easy to pay the tax liabilities currently owed by having a "liability by payroll item" report on its "reports" menu and a "pay tax liabilities" selection on its "activities" menu under "payroll." Figure 9-10 shows the payroll liability report for federal withholding for the month of December for our sample company. Notice that $950 is owed to the federal government for income taxes withheld during December, with a breakdown of employees' individual liabilities.

Figure 9-10: *Sample tax liability report*

Rock Castle Construction
Transactions by Payroll Liability Item
As of December 14, 1995

Type	Date	Num	Name	Amount	Balance
Federal Withholding					0.00
Paycheck	9/30/95	827	Joel T Brown	443.00	443.00
Paycheck	9/30/95	828	Peter J Miller	456.00	899.00
Liability Check	10/15/95	Phone trans	Great Statewide Bank	-899.00	0.00
Paycheck	10/31/95	850	Joel T Brown	439.00	439.00
Paycheck	10/31/95	851	Peter J Miller	511.00	950.00
Liability Check	11/15/95	Phone trans	Great Statewide Bank	-950.00	0.00
Paycheck	11/30/95	873	Joel T Brown	439.00	439.00
Paycheck	11/30/95	874	Peter J Miller	511.00	950.00
Total Federal Withholding				950.00	950.00
TOTAL				**950.00**	**950.00**

Paying that tax liability is extremely easy: Figure 9-11 shows the "liability check" screen that appears when you choose to "pay tax liabilities." When I selected the payee on this screen (Great Statewide Bank), the last check I wrote to that payee appeared; all I had to do was change the amount to $950 owed

December 15 for federal withholding and enter amounts for the other federal taxes. When this check is recorded in the general ledger accounts, the federal withholding liability account will be debited (decreased) and cash will be credited (decreased). A similar procedure is followed when it is time to pay state income taxes, federal and state unemployment taxes, and the other contributions and deductions that are withheld from employee earnings.

Figure 9-11: *Sample entry for paying tax liabilities*

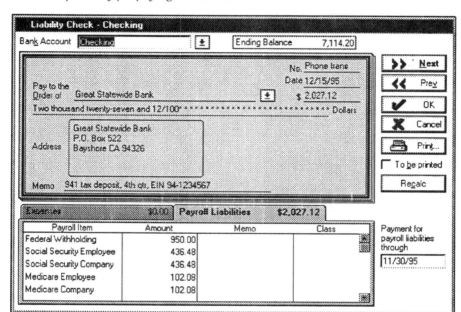

Saving and Backing Up Your Data

We have spent a lot of time on payroll setup, and as the year rolls by, you will prepare a lot of payroll checks. Don't take a chance on losing all that hard work by allowing a computer crash (or some natural disaster) to ruin your day by not having a backup copy of the payroll files to rely on. The process of backing up all of your accounting data is so important that it should be done each day. Please be sure to make a backup copy of your accounting files just after you set up your payroll master files and after each payroll period. See Chapter 2 for specifics on some backup procedures.

Chapter Ten

Payroll Reports

Introduction to Payroll Reports

Even though the most important report from a payroll module is the paycheck, there are numerous other reports available that can help you maintain effective control over salary and payroll tax expenses. These payroll reports focus either on the employee, the company account affected by a payday, or the taxes that result from a payroll. Since many of the deductions that you make from employee paychecks must be held temporarily and then paid to taxing agencies or insurance companies, you want to be very sure that these payments are timely and accurate. Payroll journals, employee earnings records, listings of the employee master file, and tax liability reports are all output that contribute to your control of wage and salary administration. This chapter introduces you to a variety of Payroll reports so you can choose which ones are most relevant to your business.

Where previous chapters described general ledger, accounts receivable, and accounts payable reports, it was explained that it is possible to customize the reports that are offered by the software packages. Payroll modules also provide you with the ability to customize existing reports in a way that suits you. Once you view a payroll report, you can delete rows or columns, add rows or columns, specify your own headings, and request various levels of subtotals.

Let's get started on the path to your effective use of payroll reports so that you can be assured you are paying your employees correctly and are satisfying government tax laws as well.

Getting the Printed Results

Most accounting software packages will have a "reports" icon and/or main menu item labeled "reports," with "general ledger, accounts payable, accounts receivable, and payroll" as report categories within that menu. QuickBooks places the printing of lists and forms under the "file, print" menu in addition to having the traditional "reports" menu. One-Write Plus has a "print" selection under the "entries" menu that leads to the printing of checks, invoices, statements, and labels, but choosing "employee" under their "reports" menu will produce a list of payroll reports. When you select payroll reports, you will be faced with many report choices.

List of Payroll Reports

Here is a list of the most widely available payroll reports:

- company payroll master file
- employee mailing labels
- employee master file list
- employee master list with earnings record
- payroll check register
- payroll detail by employee
- payroll journal
- payroll liabilities
- payroll summary by employee
- W-2 and W-3 Forms
- 940 report and/or forms
- 941 report and/or forms

Make your choice from the reports list and you will be prompted to specify some customizing choices like the period of time to include and some "filtering criteria." Using filtering criteria (like selecting only hourly employees and excluding all other types of employees) gives you the power to design finely tuned reports that better fit your needs. You should also be able to specify whether you want the reports displayed on-screen or printed immediately.

Some of these payroll reports are absolutely necessary to the functioning of your business, and some are optional but may help you manage better. Let's take a look at the most important of these reports.

Absolutely Necessary Reports

The printed results of processing accomplished by your computer is called the audit trail (explained in detail in Chapter 3). The payroll audit trail includes documents like time cards (if you use them) and the printed output that gives evidence that you have paid your employees and have recorded the appropriate payroll taxes and deductions. For example, you should produce and keep a copy of the employee pay stub (the details of gross pay, deductions, and additions) as you write the paychecks. When an employee is paid, two transactions are recorded in the accounting records; one for the employee paycheck and one for the employer's portion of appropriate payroll taxes (this was covered in detail in Chapter 9). At the very least, you will want to have a written record of these two transactions for each employee in the payroll journal. These items constitute a minimum audit trail for payroll.

Necessary for Your Employees

Paychecks

You probably don't need any further explanation of what a paycheck is. Chapter 9 provided the details of its preparation and showed the contents of the payroll check in Figure 9-9. The paycheck itself should be accompanied by a perforated tear-off section, usually referred to as the pay stub, that provides the details of gross pay, deductions, and net pay for both the current pay period and year-to-date totals. Figure 10-1 provides a sample of this type of paycheck from QuickBooks.

Figure 10-1: *Sample paycheck*

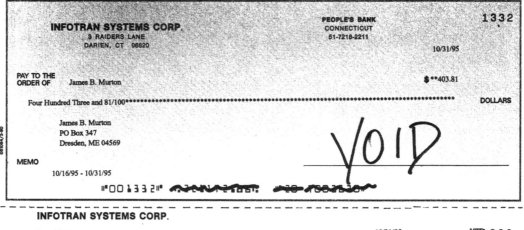

In Figure 10-1, please notice that the names of the payroll items that were set up in the company default file (federal withholding, Medicare employee, pension plan, etc.) become the deduction categories on the pay stub. You can see why it is important for these payroll item names to be as full and descriptive as possible. It is also possible to report sick and vacation days on the QuickBooks pay stub as shown in the lower left corner of the figure.

If you want to print paychecks automatically with your payroll module, you will have to order check forms (with magnetic coding for your bank account) that include a perforated section for the tear-off pay stub. The paycheck shown in Figure 10-1 actually has two duplicate pay stubs so you can tear off the lower stub to retain for company files (not shown in the figure), while the upper stub remains attached to the check for the employee.

W-2 Wage and Tax Statement

The W-2 wage and tax statement that is required for each employee at the end of the year is covered in the "year-end closing" section later in this chapter.

Necessary For Management Control

Payroll Journal

The payroll journal is your written record of the postings that have been made to general ledger accounts as a result of writing paychecks. This report should be printed for each pay period and be arranged in order by employee name or number. It includes the gross pay, deductions, and net pay, as well as the amounts for employer payroll tax and deductions liabilities. (Refer to Chapter 9 if you need a review of these transactions and the effect they have on the general ledger accounts.) Because this report is a journal, it will show the payroll transaction amounts in debits and credits. An example from Peachtree is shown in Figure 10-2.

Figure 10-2: *Sample payroll journal*

JAN'S JUMPING SERVICE Payroll Journal For the Period From Feb 15, 1994 to Feb 15, 1994					
Date Employee	GL Acct ID	GL Acct Description	Reference	Debit Amt	Credit Amt
2/15/94	62500	Wages Expense	0108	1,000.00	
Karen Walton	23100	Feder W/H Tax Payable			40.00
	23120	FICA Employer Tax Payable			62.00
	23125	Medicare Employer Tax Payable			14.50
	23200	State W/H Tax Payable			9.67
	23120	FICA Employer Tax Payable			62.00
	23125	Medicare Employer Tax Payable			14.50
	25100	FUTA Payable			8.00
	24100	SUTA Payable			0.30
	75400	Employer Payroll Tax Expense		62.00	
	75400	Employer Payroll Tax Expense		14.50	
	75400	Employer Payroll Tax Expense		8.00	
	75400	Employer Payroll Tax Expense		0.30	
	10100	Regular Checking Account			873.83
2/15/94	62500	Wages Expense	0109	400.00	
Phil Jagobender	23100	Feder W/H Tax Payable			52.57
	23120	FICA Employer Tax Payable			24.80
	23125	Medicare Employer Tax Payable			5.80
	23200	State W/H Tax Payable			20.66

(this is a partial report)

An examination of the transaction for Karen Walton in this figure allows us to better understand the purpose of the payroll journal. The first debit in this figure is the gross pay (wages expense), while the last credit is the net pay. All of the amounts deducted from the employee paycheck, as well as the employer taxes, are credited to payable accounts. The amounts debited to employer payroll tax expense are the employer portion of FICA, Medicare, federal unemployment, and state unemployment taxes. The important use of this journal is to identify the general ledger accounts that were affected by the payroll transactions.

The payroll journal in One-Write Plus is similar to Figure 10-2. Unfortunately, QuickBooks does not provide for a payroll journal. It is possible, and quite worthwhile, to design a customized report by displaying an individual employee paycheck on screen and then requesting a "transaction journal" from the "reports" menu. You would need to do this, however, for each employee, each pay period, printing one page at a time; a rather cumbersome routine.

Payroll Check Register

Some businesses write their payroll checks using their regular checking account, and some of them use a separate account for payroll checks. If you use a separate account to issue all paychecks, it is a good practice to print a payroll check register for each pay period. This register is a list of check numbers and payees, with the check amount being the employee net pay. This lets you quickly check to see that all check numbers are accounted for and that the total amount being paid is reasonable compared to previous pay periods. Figure 10-3 provides an example from Peachtree of the payroll check register. You can see that this report gives no details for each employee and no account numbers, so it does not replace the payroll journal. It is most commonly used to check off the cleared checks in order to make a list of outstanding checks for the bank statement reconciliation process.

Figure 10-3: *Sample payroll check register*

<table>
<tr><td colspan="4" align="center">**Bellweather Cleaning Services**
Payroll Check Register
For the Period From Mar 15, 1995 to Mar 15, 1995</td></tr>
<tr><td>**Reference**</td><td>**Date**</td><td>**Employee**</td><td>**Amount**</td></tr>
<tr><td>2200</td><td>3/15/95</td><td>Steve Wayne Austin</td><td>314.86</td></tr>
<tr><td>2201</td><td>3/15/95</td><td>Felicia Kessler</td><td>330.06</td></tr>
<tr><td>2202</td><td>3/15/95</td><td>Kay J. Guillatt</td><td>348.11</td></tr>
<tr><td>2203</td><td>3/15/95</td><td>Abbey Moore</td><td>200.91</td></tr>
<tr><td>2204</td><td>3/15/95</td><td>Patti Rose Tremont</td><td>252.51</td></tr>
<tr><td></td><td></td><td></td><td>1,446.45</td></tr>
</table>

If you print your payroll checks from your regular checking account (where you also write checks to vendors), then printing a check register (as described in Chapter 8) is all that is needed. This one check register will include your employee paychecks.

The Employee Earnings Record

The Employee Master File (as discussed in the previous chapter) holds all the permanent data about an employee. This includes social security number, federal tax filing status, pay rate, location, home address, etc. In Peachtree, QuickBooks, and One-Write Plus, this Employee Master File also holds all the paycheck data for each employee throughout the year. In other words, the employee master file serves as the employee earnings record and contains the details of payments to each employee. Figure 10-4 from One-Write Plus displays an employee master record that includes the payroll history for one employee from the beginning of the year through the current date.

Figure 10-4: *Employee master record with earnings history*

The Kite Store
EMPLOYEE CARD REPORT
Jones, Mike

EMPLOYEE ID: JONES

CATEGORY: Full Time

ADDRESS:
Mike Jones
4 Iroquois Circle
Apartment 17G
Breezy, MA 123451234
Phone: (603) 880-1234
Department: Ext: 111111
Social Security #: 001-98-2644

Pay Type: HOURLY
Status: Active
Married Status: Single
Pay Frequency: Semi-monthly

PERSONNEL DATA:
Date of Birth: 4/23/70
Date of Hire: 4/3/90
Termination Date:

Previous Pay: $9.00
Last Review Date: 12/30/95
Next Review Date: 12/30/96

Accrued Vacation: 30.00
Accrued Sick: 12.00

COMMENTS:

EMPLOYEE HISTORY

DATE	REF NO	TOT HRS	GROSS PAY	WITHHOLDINGS	DEDUCTIONS	NET PAY
01/15/96	00000234	40.00	400.00	87.89	38.20	273.91
01/31/96	00000237	42.00	430.00	95.90	39.70	294.40
02/15/96	00000240	40.00	400.00	87.89	38.20	273.91
02/29/96	00000243	40.00	400.00	87.89	38.20	273.91
3/15/96	00000246	40.00	400.00	87.89	38.20	273.91
3/29/96	00000249	50.00	550.00	128.00	45.70	376.30

The one shortcoming of the report in Figure 10-4 is that it does not provide subtotals by month or quarter. QuickBooks provides a payroll summary by employee (see "quarterly reports" later in this chapter) that does provide quarterly totals by employee, but doesn't break those totals down into pay periods. Obviously, you need to choose which detail is most important to you in order to pick the right accounting software for your business.

Other Useful Payroll Reports

Employee Master List

The employee master card in Figure 10-4 shows the full contents of the record for just one employee. The contents of the permanent information in a master file might also be printed in list format. A listing from the master file could be as simple as a telephone directory that listed only the name, department, and company phone number, or as elaborate as one that contained every bit of permanent information in the file. The employee master list in Figure 10-5 from Peachtree is comprehensive. It shows all the fields in the master file for every employee. Without customization, this list prints each field in a separate column across three pieces of paper. I customized it to squeeze the data into the format for this book, with the fields stacked three deep.

Figure 10-5: *Sample employee master list*

		Jan's Jumping Service Employee Master List			
Employee ID Employee	Address line 1 Address line 2 City ST ZIP	SS No Fed Filing Status Pay Type	Fed Allow ST Filing Status Pension	Hire Date Frequency Desc 1	G/L Acct 1 Hrly/Sal 1
DIEHL Timothy A. Diehl	PO Box 400 75 Back Road Kingfield, ME 04988 Franklin	155-89-6332 Married Hourly	2 Married Yes	2/16/94 Weekly Regular	62500 16.00
JG-SR James Gutmann, VEEP	745 Paine Avenue New Vineyard, ME 04950 Somer	455-89-7887 Single Salaried	1 Single No	8/20/93 Monthly Salary	62500 3,000.00
KW-SP Karen Walton	100 Janeway Road Box 606 Saco, ME 04123 York	133-35-8996 Married Salaried	1 Married Yes	1/1/94 Monthly Salary	62500 1,000.00

(this is a partial report)

The employee master list needs to be printed after a pay rate change. This may be done after every change or periodically—the goal is to update this file. Since the data in the file is relatively permanent, there is no need to print its content each pay period.

Employee Mailing Labels

It is not as common to need mailing labels for employees as it is for vendors or customers, but the capability is there. Whenever you have stored a set of names and addresses, you can print mailing labels. Of course, you might need mailing labels for all your employees to mail W-2 Forms at year-end or for special announcements. Peachtree, QuickBooks, and One-Write Plus can print mailing labels in various order (by zip code for example) and for a type of employee (like hourly or salaried). Look for "mailing labels" on the payroll report menu of Peachtree, on the "print forms, mailing labels" selection in QuickBooks, or on the "entries, print, labels, employees" menu selections of One-Write Plus. Check the user's manual to see what options are available for size and style of labels.

Payroll Tax Liability Report

The purpose of a tax liability report is to list the tax liabilities that were generated during a specific payroll period or that were generated by all the payroll transactions for a period of time like a month or quarter. This report should specify a date, the gross amount of the payroll, and a list of the amount of tax associated with that gross pay (e.g., the FICA and Medicare tax). One-Write Plus and Peachtree produce a tax liability report that includes the taxable gross pay for any specific date, or range of dates, that you identify. Figure 10-6 provides an example from One-Write Plus.

Figure 10-6: *Payroll tax liability listing*

The Kite Store
PAYROLL TAX LIABILITY REPORT
3/15/96 TO 3/15/96

	Taxable Wages	Tax Withheld
Total wages, tips and other compensation	1,625.00	
FEDERAL TAX		
Wages subject to Federal income tax withheld	1,625.00	
Total Federal income tax withheld		171.88
Wages subject to Medicare tax withheld	1,625.00	
Total Medicare tax withheld		23.56
Total employer's share		23.56
Wages subject to Social Security tax withheld	1,625.00	
Total Social Security tax withheld		100.75
Total employer's share		100.75
TOTAL FEDERAL TAX LIABILITY		420.50
STATE TAX		
Wages subject to State MA Income Tax	1,625.00	
Total State MA Income Tax withheld		80.53

(this is a partial report)

Notice in Figure 10-6 that this listing reports the total gross pay for all employees for a March 15 pay date and then lists the amount of taxes that were calculated on that gross pay for that date. Although state income taxes are listed here, you might notice that this report will not include deductions made for health insurance, dental insurance, pension plans, and other special deductions (since they are not taxes). If this report is printed for each pay period, the amounts from the pay period reports can be accumulated for a month or quarter to be matched to the quarterly tax reports discussed in the next section.

Alternatively, Figure 10-7 provides the QuickBooks version of the tax liability report. This report, dated "As of December 14," shows the ending balance in the payroll liability accounts at that date. These amounts reflect the deductions recorded since the last time the taxes were paid to the appropriate taxing agencies, because these liability accounts also reflect the payments made. QuickBooks does not offer a report of payroll liabilities that includes gross pay or covers one payroll period or a range of dates.

Figure 10-7: *Payroll liabilities as of a specific date*

	Dec 14, '95
Rock Castle Construction	
Liabilities by Payroll Item	
As of December 14, 1995	
Payroll Liabilities	
Federal Withholding	950.00
Medicare Employee	102.08
Social Security Employee	436.48
Federal Unemployment	0.00
Medicare Company	102.08
Social Security Company	436.48
CA - Withholding	0.00
CA - Disability Employee	0.00
CA - Unemployment Company	0.00
Health Insurance	-190.00
CA Employment Training Tax	0.00
Total Payroll Liabilities	**1,837.12**

More about Tax Reports and Requirements

The previous chapter introduced the basic categories of taxes and payroll deductions that are mandated by federal and municipal agencies. Because these tax obligations are regulated by law, there are a few reports and forms that you must file with federal and local government agencies. The most widely recognized of these is the annual W-2, sent to each employee. Employers also must report quarterly, and sometimes even monthly wages and taxes due on IRS Form 941. Your payroll software will help you prepare these forms. An overview of this process follows.

Quarterly Reports

IRS Form 941 is called the "employers quarterly federal tax return." Although you may have to remit federal payroll taxes on a monthly or even weekly basis using a payment coupon, you will only have to file Form 941 at the end of each quarter. A discussion of the tax deposit and filing requirements is beyond the scope of this book, but accounting software provides the information that will help you comply with these laws.

Form 941

Peachtree includes the capability of producing a federal Form 941, while One-Write Plus and QuickBooks produce a quarterly report that includes all the information needed to fill in Form 941. In general, this form or report lists the total gross wages earned by your employees that is taxable for purposes of calculating federal income tax withholding, FICA, Medicare, and federal unemployment taxes. Most states require a withholding form that mirrors the federal form. The appropriate tax rates are applied to gross wages, and the amount of tax in each of these categories is reported. Any amounts that were deposited to pay these taxes are also reported on this form; and the net amount due is calculated. Figure 10-8 shows a Form 941 for one quarter completed by the Peachtree payroll module.

Figure 10-8: *Sample quarterly 941 Form*

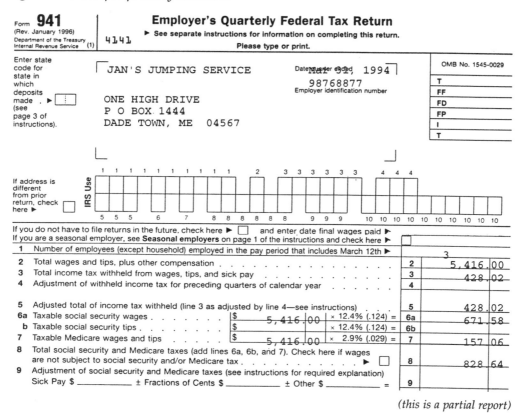

(this is a partial report)

Although One-Write Plus and QuickBooks do not actually print data on the Form 941, they both provide a quarterly report of gross wages and payroll taxes that list the exact figures you need to fill in the federal form. For example, Figure 10-9 illustrates the quarterly summary from One-Write Plus. In this figure, you will notice the gross pay and tax totals for the quarter in the far right column that can be placed in appropriate fields on the Form 941. The totals on this report also allow you to see the total quarterly obligations to remit amounts to your pension plan administrator, health insurance agency, and local charitable contributions agencies.

Figure 10-9: *Sample quarterly report with 941 information*

The Kite Store		
941 QUARTERLY REPORT		
1/1/96 To 3/31/96		

Total wages, tips, and other compensation		10,101.00
Total income tax withheld		1,083.92
Taxable Social Security wages	10,101.00 x 12.40% = 1,252.52	
Taxable Social Security tips	0.00 x 12.40% = 0.00	
Taxable Medicare wages and tips	10,101.00 x 2.90% = 292.93	
Total Social Security and Medicare taxes		1,545.45
Advanced earned income credit (EIC) payments made to employees		0.00
Monthly Summary of Federal Tax Liability:		
First month liability	849.64	
Second month liability	859.19	
Third month liability	920.54	
Total liability for the quarter		2,629.37

Annual Payroll Requirements

Even if you have not been printing the employee pay history from your employee master file as described earlier in this chapter, you will want to print some form of comprehensive listing of payroll activity for each employee at the end of the year. I would suggest the type of employee history that was shown in Figure 10-4 earlier in this chapter, or an annual summary like the quarterly one of Figure 10-9. The annual totals of gross pay and tax deductions for each employee must, by law, be reported to the IRS and to the employee on a W-2 wage and tax statement. In addition, you will be required to file a W-3 Form (the employer's summary of the W-2's for all your employees), plus a Form 940 (the annual summary of FUTA tax). Again, all accounting software has the capability to provide the information you will need to file these forms.

W-2 Wage and Tax Statement

Peachtree can print the annual results directly on the W-2 Forms provided by the IRS or purchased from an office supply source. Figure 10-10 is an example of a W-2 Form prepared by Peachtree. Although this is a federal form, please notice that the state income tax withheld is reported at the bottom. Each of the W-2 Forms should be matched (sometimes called reconciled) to the annual summary for the employee to ensure accuracy of the wage and tax amounts. A group of W-2 Forms is followed by a summary listing of the W-2s to be used in the preparation of a W-3 summary.

Alternatively, One-Write Plus and QuickBooks provide the data in a convenient report form for filling out the W-2s. Figure 10-11 shows an example of this from One-Write Plus. Figure 10-11 shows the data for just the first two employees; at the end of this report, you would find a summary page (not shown) that is labeled "W-3 Summary."

Figure 10-10: *Sample W-2 Form prepared by payroll system*

a Control number gut1	22222	Void ☐	For Official Use Only ► OMB No. 1545-0008			
b Employer's identification number 98768877				**1** Wages, tips, other compensation 2816.00		**2** Federal income tax withheld 279.95
c Employer's name, address, and ZIP code JAN'S JUMPING SERVICE ONE HIGH DRIVE P O BOX 1444 DADE TOWN. ME 04567				**3** Social security wages 2816.00		**4** Social security tax withheld 174.59
				5 Medicare wages and tips 2816.00		**6** Medicare tax withheld 40.83
				7 Social security tips		**8** Allocated tips
d Employee's social security number 133456789				**9** Advance EIC payment		**10** Dependent care benefits
e Employee's name (first, middle initial, last) Jean Gutmann				**11** Nonqualified plans		**12** Benefits included in box 1
P O Box 34 Kingfield, ME 04947 Franklin				**13** See Instrs. for box 13		**14** Other
f Employee's address and ZIP code				**15** Statutory employee ☐ Deceased ☐ Pension plan ☐ Legal rep. ☐ Hshld. emp. ☐ Subtotal ☐ Deferred compensation ☐		
16 State Employer's state I.D. No. ME 98768877-2		**17** State wages, tips, etc. 2816.00	**18** State income tax 91.95	**19** Locality name	**20** Local wages, tips, etc.	**21** Local income tax

41-852411   APR. I.R.S.   Department of the Treasury – Internal Revenue Service

Form **W-2** Wage and Tax Statement **1995**

Copy A For Social Security Administration

Figure 10-11: *Sample W-2 annual summary report*

The Kite Store
W-2 REPORT
1996

Employer: The Kite Store   Company Tax ID:
            119 Breezy Avenue
            P.O. Box 2
            Windswept, MA 00000

EMPLOYEE/SS#	BOX	NAME	AMOUNT
Mike Jones			
4 Iroquois Circle			
Apartment 17G			
Breezy, MA 12345			
001-98-2644			
	1	Wages, tips, other compensation	2,451.00
	2	Federal income tax withheld	271.10
	3	Social Security wages	2,451.00
	4	Social Security tax withheld	151.97
	5	Medicare wages and tips	2,451.00
	6	Medicare tax withheld	35.54
	13	D	129.00
	14	Medical	64.50
	14	Dental	44.70
	15		Deferred Comp
	16	State/Employer's State ID	MA
	16	State/Employer's State ID	
	17	State Wage	2,451.00
	18	State income tax	116.85
Michelle Smith			
75 Main Street			
Breezy, MA 12345			
003-00-7475			
	1	Wages, tips, other compensation	900.00
	2	Federal income tax withheld	38.46
	3	Social Security wages	900.00
	4	Social Security tax withheld	55.80

(this is a partial report)

Form 940

Most employers will pay both a federal and a state unemployment tax and will file a Form 940 at year-end for each of these. Although low-end software will not fill in a Form 940, the information you need for this form is readily available on a year-end summary. The report needs to contain the total gross wages for the year, the taxable gross wages under unemployment tax law (remember that gross wages for each employee are taxable only up to $7,000), and the amount of FUTA or SUTA owed. You may have deposited some unemployment taxes as the year progressed, and this is reported on Form 940 to determine the amount owed at year-end. Figure 10-12 shows an example of the unemployment tax summary provided by One-Write Plus, which provides the data needed for Form 940.

Figure 10-12: *Sample annual summary for Form 940*

	The Kite Store		
	940 ANNUAL FUTA REPORT		
	1/1/96 TO 12/31/96		

	FUTA BASIS	Gross	
	FUTA LIMIT	7,000.00	
	FUTA %	0.80000	

QUARTER	TOTAL WAGES	EXCESS WAGES	TAXABLE WAGES
FIRST QUARTER	10,980.00	500.00	10,480.00
SECOND QUARTER	11,010.00	7,500.00	3,510.00
THIRD QUARTER	10,570.00	7,890.00	2,680.00
FOURTH QUARTER	11,910.00	11,070.00	840.00
	44,470.00	26,960.00	17,510.00
			0.80000%
TOTAL DUE			140.08

Year-End Closing Procedures for Payroll

Since it is crucial that you accumulate wage records that start at zero for each employee at the beginning of a year, you must be sure to "close" your payroll records at the end of a year. This payroll closing process removes the year-to-date earnings amounts from each employee's record. Even though most accounting packages do not require you to close the general ledger, or customer ledger, or vendor ledger at the end of the year, closing the payroll records is a special procedure. First, be sure that you have printed any annual payroll summary reports you will need, along with the appropriate federal forms. Then use the instructions in the user's manual for your software to close the payroll year.

What to Save/What to Ignore

Your payroll module will probably produce many more reports than you will ever need. When you first start working with a payroll system, it is a good idea to experiment with all the various reports that the module provides and match the information provided on the reports with your needs and personal preferences.

Try to keep in mind that your business history is represented by your accounting reports. Choose among the available reports with comparability in mind; that is, print reports on a periodic basis that can be compared to previous periods for reasonableness and accuracy. Filing requirements within the states where you do business will also dictate which reports you should print on a regular basis. Experience will tell you what is necessary and what is excess.

My recommendation for the minimum set of payroll reports to be printed and filed for each period in a book or folder is:

- employee master record with earnings history (or a copy of the pay stub for each employee)
- payroll journal
- payroll tax liability report
- quarterly summary report

If you are a large enough business that you are required to deposit tax amounts to the federal or state collection points on a weekly or monthly basis, then the printing of a payroll tax liability report and payroll summary report should be as frequent as the time period for which you must pay these obligations.

Exporting Payroll Data to Other Software

You will probably find many reasons why you would want to use some set of data from your payroll system in another computer activity like applications for health insurance benefits or special personnel mailings to employees. The procedure for exporting payroll data is similar to that for exporting general ledger or accounts payable data (refer to Chapters 4, 6, and 8 for examples of this process). While exporting can be fairly complex, the information you gain may help you manage your business more efficiently.

Disclaimer about Payroll Laws

The discussions in this chapter have been aimed at helping you understand the payroll process and its reports with no intent to be a comprehensive guide to payroll tax laws. If you are preparing and paying your own payroll, you must seek expert advice from an accountant to be sure you are complying with local and federal laws. The author and publisher assume no responsibility for the accuracy or completeness of the tax rates and tax laws that have been referred to in this chapter.

Chapter Eleven

Inventory Management

Introduction to the Inventory Function

Inventory Management is all of the procedures and activities related to buying, selling, and controlling inventory. Inventory can be merchandise that is purchased in finished condition for resale, or it could be raw materials, items in the process of being assembled, or finished goods inventory resulting from a manufacturing process. In order to keep the presentation in this chapter within a reasonable scope, the term "inventory" will refer only to merchandise in stock that was purchased for resale.

When a company tracks this inventory, it records all purchases of goods in an asset account, usually titled "merchandise inventory," and then reduces this account whenever goods are sold. Since the selling price is recorded as sales revenue and cash (or accounts receivable if the sale is on account), the cost of the goods that are sold must be deducted from inventory and recorded in an expense account, usually titled "cost of goods sold" or "cost of sales." Periodically, you will want to review your inventory records to determine what needs to be reordered and to get a picture of the profitability of your sales as they relate to your inventory items. The most basic inventory reports include a stock status report, a reorder report, a cost analysis report, and a sales analysis report.

This topic needs a whole book to itself! Many small business accounting packages do not provide a full inventory management module—they simply can't do it because the aspects of inventory control are so vast. Peachtree for Windows does the best job of providing sophisticated inventory management, with QuickBooks coming in second. One-Write Plus includes a quantity tracking

Note: The accrual basis of accounting is assumed in the discussions in this chapter. See Chapter 3 for an explanation of accrual based accounting.

inventory module that does not apply a unit cost; providing only an inventory item list (inventory cards) but no function for tracking cost of goods sold or inventory profitability. Consequently, this chapter showcases only the Peachtree and QuickBooks inventory functions. Even if you do not need to manage inventory in the traditional sense of the word, you will probably want to keep a list of the items (or service categories) that you sell, so read on.

Perpetual vs. Periodic Inventory Systems

In a perpetual inventory system, transactions involving the purchase and sale of merchandise are recorded continually as they occur. In this way, an inventory ledger (or card file) is kept constantly up to date. Purchases of inventory are recorded by increasing the asset account entitled inventory, which is the summary account for the inventory ledger. When inventory is sold, two entries are necessary: one to reduce the inventory account by the cost of the goods that are sold and one to record the revenue earned from the sale.

The alternative to the perpetual system is called the periodic inventory system. In a periodic system, the inventory account is not updated with sales and purchases, and no cost of goods sold is recorded at the time of sales. Rather, the inventory account is updated only at the end of a period (usually the end of the year), and that update is based solely on a physical count of inventory. The inventory module of a computerized accounting system is intended to allow small businesses to employ the perpetual system of control. Consequently, this chapter will focus only on perpetual inventory systems.

Cost vs. Price

There can be considerable confusion over the meaning of the terms "cost" and "price." The cost of an item is the dollar amount that you paid to acquire the item. The price is the dollar amount you charge when you sell that item. Please keep these definitions in mind as you read this chapter. While we are on the topic of cost and price, let's learn another important accounting term: gross margin. The gross margin earned on an item (sometimes called gross profit) is the difference between its price and its cost.

Input, Processing, and Output of an Inventory System

QuickBooks provides a QuickTour of its software features that includes a handy reference to their inventory module. Figure 11-1 from this QuickTour provides a view in a nutshell of the major inputs to an inventory system. From this illustration, you can see that data from the new item record (this is the inventory master file) is used when additional inventory is ordered on a purchase order, or purchased directly by writing a check, and the item data is also used when a sales invoice is created. In other words, the purchase and sale of items constitute the main input for an inventory system.

Figure 11-1: *Inventory components from QuickTour*

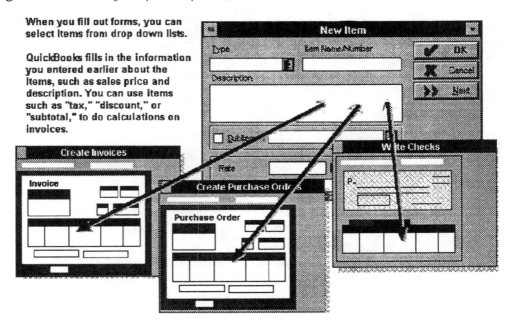

Figure 11-2 provides a more detailed picture of the input and output from an inventory system and provides the framework for the rest of this chapter. You will be able to understand the components and the processing that goes on behind the scenes if we can walk through this flowchart together.

Input

From the flowchart in Figure 11-2, you can see that in addition to purchases and sales, the inventory master file and infrequent inventory adjustments serve as the inputs to an inventory system. The inventory master file contains the permanent record of item numbers, descriptions, units, costs, and prices. Purchase orders for inventory are initiated by the inventory system itself (notice the flow line returning to the top of this chart from the end of the processing steps) and would be marked for payment when the items in the purchase order are received. Purchase orders and the purchase invoices received directly from vendors are actually processed within the accounts payable (AP) module using data from the inventory master file. As sales transactions are recorded in the accounts receivable (AR) module, data is retrieved from the inventory master file in order to calculate amounts and post (copy the amounts) to the ledgers. Inventory adjustments might be necessary for a miscount of items, goods returned, lost or stolen items, or cost/price changes; and are almost always needed after a physical count is taken.

Most of the input to an inventory system happens automatically during the transaction entries of the accounts payable and accounts receivable systems. The creation and maintenance of the inventory master file is the most crucial step, and this file is covered in detail in the next section of this chapter.

Figure 11-2: *Inventory data flow*

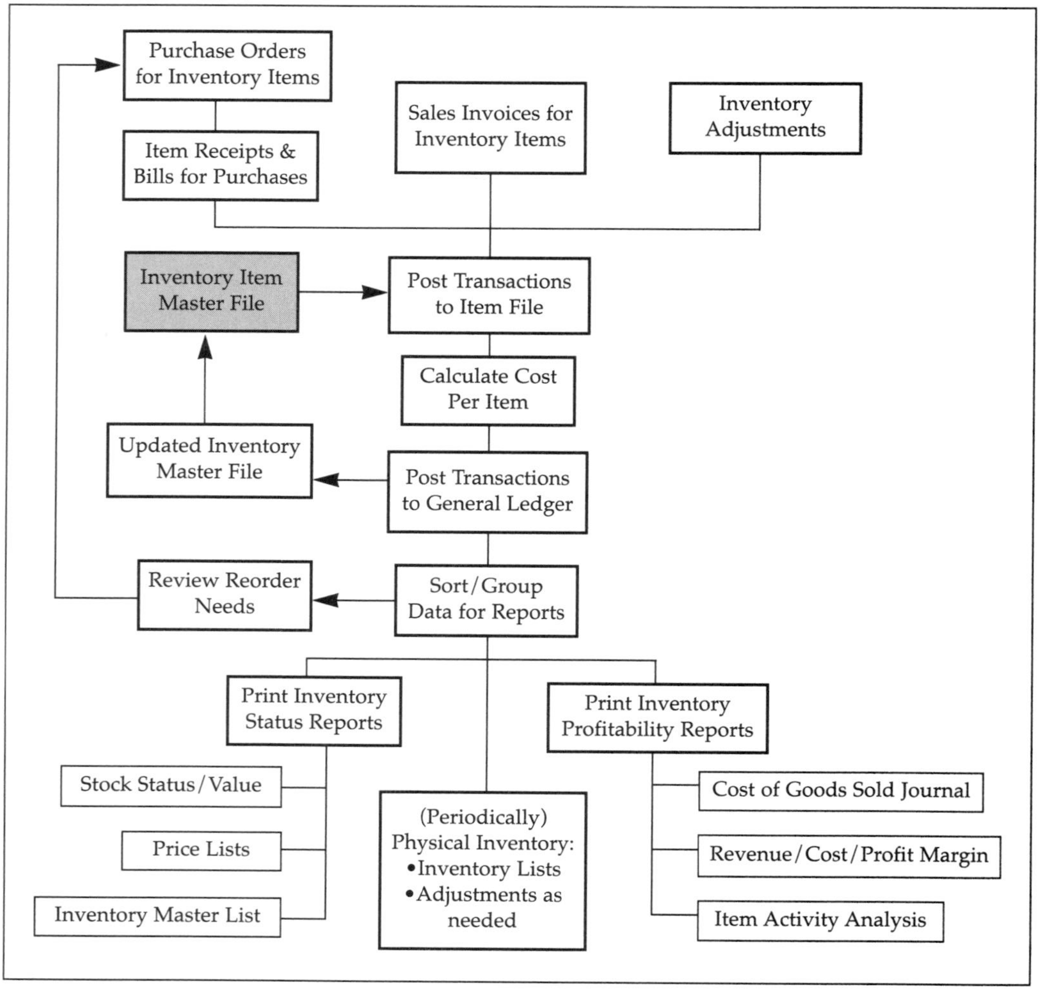

Processing

The processing steps named in the flowchart of Figure 11-2 are those actions that take place to update the inventory master file and the general ledger (GL). The new balance of an inventory item (its current "status") must be determined—that is, any purchases, sales, and adjustments must be added to or subtracted from the previous balance of items in inventory. As this posting (copying) of transactions occurs, the computer will recalculate the current cost of the item based on all purchase and adjustment data that is now contained within the record for each item. Most small business accounting packages will calculate an average cost of the item based on the history for that item (see "inventory costing methods" later in this chapter).

All inventory transactions affect accounts in the general ledger and must be posted (copied) to those GL accounts. For example, when a purchase of inventory is recorded in the accounts payable system, it will be posted to the general ledger as an increase in the inventory account and as an increase in accounts payable—we'll get to the debit and credit business in a minute. The final processing step is the sorting and grouping of data in order to produce the reports you want. For example, the inventory master file would need to be searched to find items where the quantity in stock has fallen below the required minimum level for that item so a reorder report can be created.

Output

The inventory function of your accounting software should produce two major types of output: reports informing you of the current status of your inventory and reports aimed at helping you track the profitability of holding and selling that inventory. The stock status report is simply a list of all items in inventory indicating the number of units of each item in stock and the status of any outstanding purchase orders. A total cost for each item and a total on this report tells you the total valuation of your inventory and can be matched to the ending balance in the inventory asset account in the general ledger. It is helpful to have a price list within easy reach of anyone who sells your product: this can be as simple as an item list (alphabetical by item name) with the selling price for each item, or as comprehensive as a sales catalog that includes number of items in stock with sizes, colors, and locations. The inventory master list is a printout of all the data in your inventory master file.

You can review the additions to inventory by studying the purchases journal produced by your accounts payable module, but to review the deductions in inventory, you will need a cost of goods sold journal. This report details the general ledger postings that result from all sales of inventory items. An inventory profit margin report lets you view the quantity sold, total sales revenue, cost of goods sold, and gross profit for each item in inventory. (The inventory profit margin will help make such management decisions as which items to feature and which to drop from inventory.) The item activity analysis report shows the beginning quantity, purchases, sales, adjustments, and ending quantity for each item to help you determine which items are the movers and which are the sleepers.

When you are ready to take a physical inventory (described later in this chapter) it is helpful to have a worksheet listing all items in inventory, with their description (and location, if possible) and a blank line for the actual count. Peachtree and QuickBooks provide this list, and you can create one with any accounting package by exporting your inventory master list to a spreadsheet.

Inventory Master File

Remember that a master file is the basic set of information about vendors, customers, employees, or inventory items that is used repeatedly in the processing of transactions. The inventory master file contains item names and descriptions, as well as other permanent information about each item that you sell.

The following are some of the items normally found in an inventory master file:

- item number
- item name and/or description
- item type (e.g., stock, nonstock, service, hardware, plumbing)
- unit of measure (e.g., gallons, pints, dozen, carton, each)
- selling price per unit (may allow several levels of sales prices)
- location of the item
- tax type for this item (e.g., sales tax, nontaxable)
- default general ledger sales account number
- default general ledger inventory account number
- default general ledger cost of sales account number
- cost per unit (calculated by the computer)
- minimum stock to keep on hand
- suggested reorder quantity and vendor

An example of a master inventory record from the Peachtree inventory master file is shown in Figure 11-3. You will notice that all of the above items are contained in this inventory entry screen and, in addition, a "custom fields" tab is available to set up data fields of your own design for things like color, size, season, target customer (e.g., toddler or teen), or shelf life. The "history" tab on the master record of Figure 11-3 allows you to view the cost and sales activity of the selected inventory item, but is for information only, since you can only accumulate this history through sales and purchase transactions. The "bill of materials" tab is used to specify the components that make up an assembly when your inventory is composed of raw material parts that are used to make a finished product. This is an advanced feature of Peachtree that is beyond the scope of this book. QuickBooks and One-Write Plus do not offer a bill of materials capability.

Figure 11-3: *Sample inventory master file record*

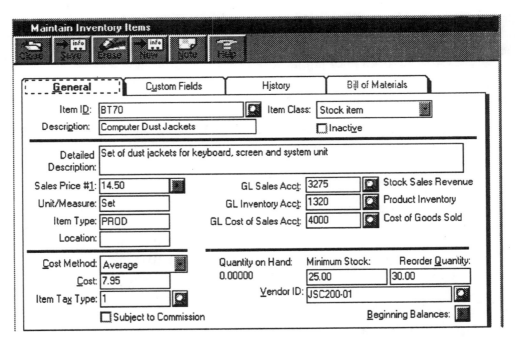

The inventory master file plays a very central role in both AP and AR processing when inventory items are being purchased or sold, because the transaction entry screens for those modules will invite you to pick an inventory item from a pop up list. This inventory list shows the items that are already contained in the inventory master file so you can select one for the current transaction. As mentioned in the previous chapters, some systems allow you to type the first few letters of an item name or number, and as soon as the computer can recognize the item, it will provide the rest of the name and any pertinent items from the master file. For example, the user need only type "compu" before the computer would recognize this inventory item as "computer dust jackets" and would display the item description and unit sales price for this item. If the inventory item is not already in the master file, the computer will notify you that the item does not exist and will encourage you to create a new record in the master file. Figure 11-3 is also the same screen that is used to create a new inventory item (notice the "new" icon on the toolbar at the top of this screen).

Inventory Ledger

The "history" tab of the inventory record that is illustrated in Figure 11-3 shows the contents of the actual inventory ledger. The inventory ledger is like a customer ledger. In other words, the master record for each item (in the master file) is used to post all the purchases, sales, and adjustments so that a running balance can be maintained for each item. When you look at the master record, you should be able to see the beginning balance, all current transactions (in and out), and an ending balance for a specific item. The contents of this file (the inventory ledger) can be reported on a detailed ledger report; QuickBooks calls it the "inventory valuation detail" (shown later in Figure 11-12), Peachtree calls it the "item costing report," and One-Write Plus uses the title "inventory activity report."

Since QuickBooks is completely "lists" oriented, it provides a very quick and helpful way to view your master inventory file (the inventory ledger) with its "item list" shown in Figure 11-4. With this list on-screen, you can easily see how many items you have in stock and what their selling price is when you have a customer on the phone. From this screen, you can also click on "QuickReport" to see the inventory ledger card (all recent activity) for a selected item. From this same screen, you may also click on "edit" to change the master record data for existing items or click on "new" to enter a new item. This illustration of the QuickBooks inventory list helps you understand the contents of the important inventory master file. Any of the QuickBooks screen displays can also be printed to paper.

Figure 11-4: *Inventory item list*

Name	Description	Type	Account	On Hand	Price
◆ Pipe	Copper pipe for pl.	Inventory Part	Sales:Materials	0	0.00
◆ 2" pipe	2 inch o.d. Coppe	Inventory Part	Sales:Materials	99	2.97
◆ 3" pipe	3 inch od Copper	Inventory Part	Sales:Materials	234	4.95
◆ 4" pipe	4 inch od Copper	Inventory Part	Sales:Materials	145	15.95
◆ Plumbing	Plumbing supplies	Inventory Part	Sales:Resale ir	0	0.00
◆ Faucet	Faucets	Inventory Part	Sales:Item sale	18	49.57
◆ Fittings	Copper Plumbing I	Inventory Part	Sales:Materials	57	17.95
◆ Sink	Sinks	Inventory Part	Sales:Item sale	-2	47.95
◆ Tape	Drywall tape	Inventory Part	Sales:Materials	70	12.50
◆ Wallboard	Gypsum wallboarc	Inventory Part	Sales:Materials	71	15.75
◆ Windows	Windows in Stock	Inventory Part	Sales:Item sale	0	0.00
◆ Bay Window	Bay Windows	Inventory Part	Sales:Item sale	3	1,250.00
◆ Std Windows	Standard size, sin.	Inventory Part	Sales:Item sale	45	42.50
◆ Concrete	Concrete, priced r	Non-inventory F	Sales:Materials		27.50
◆ Custom door	Custom ordered di	Non-inventory F	Reimbursable I		0.00
◆ Custom floor	Custom ordered flc	Non-inventory F	Reimbursable I		0.00
◆ Custom tile	Custom ordered til	Non-inventory F	Reimbursable I		95.00
◆ Custom window	Custom ordered w	Non-inventory F	Reimbursable I		0.00
◆ Light fixture	Brass ceiling fixt...	Non-inventory F	Sales:Item sale		0.00

Links with the Chart of Accounts, Accounts Payable, and Accounts Receivable

The sales and purchase transactions described earlier rely heavily on the complete list of accounts in the general ledger—called the chart of accounts and described in detail in Chapter 4. Relevant to this chapter, inventory sales and inventory purchases must also be assigned to accounts in the general ledger (GL). Peachtree, One-Write Plus, and QuickBooks require you to name default GL accounts on the inventory master record.

Take another look at Figure 11-3 and notice that default sales, inventory, and cost of sales accounts must be specified. When inventory is purchased, the software will automatically debit (increase) your inventory account (in this case, 1320, product inventory) and credit (increase) accounts payable because of the default GL accounts in the master file. When inventory is sold, the software will automatically credit (increase) the sales revenue account (in this case, account 3275, stock sales revenue) and debit (increase) cash or accounts receivable. Also, at the time of each sale, the software will automatically debit (increase) a cost of sales account (in this case, 4000, cost of goods sold) and credit (decrease) the inventory account (1320). So…naming the default GL accounts in the inventory master file allows the software to do all the background accounting work for you!

One note of caution; One-Write Plus does not track and record unit cost, so the "cost of sales" entry noted in the last paragraph is not prepared automatically by One-Write Plus.

Inventory Purchases

Reorder Reminders

Most repurchases of inventory will be triggered by the recognition that some item's stock has fallen below acceptable levels. Both Peachtree and QuickBooks have a reminder system that will display a list of issues or incidents that the software suggests you take care of—one of them is a list of inventory items that have fallen below acceptable minimum stock levels. Figure 11-5 shows an example of the Peachtree "action items" alert that lists which inventory items are low (notice the "quantity on hand below minimum stock" alert) as of the current date. The "action items" appear each time you log into your company accounting records; all you have to do is pay attention to them. Print the list shown in Figure 11-5, and you will have your reorder list. It is also possible to print a formal reorder report in QuickBooks (covered later in this chapter). Use these to prepare purchase orders for the needed inventory.

Figure 11-5: *Sample action alert for inventory*

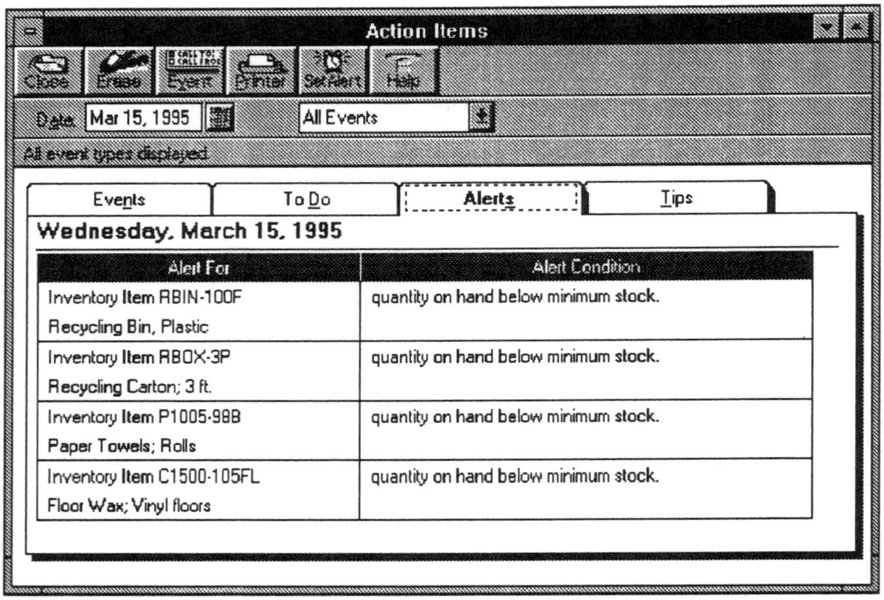

Inventory Purchase Orders

Figure 11-6 provides you with an example of an inventory purchase order transaction as it would be entered in QuickBooks. Most of the data for this purchase order is displayed automatically—all the user must do is specify the vendor, the item, and the quantity to order, and then review the other data on the screen. The unit cost ("rate") that appears on the purchase order is based on previous purchases; if the price has gone up, the vendor will notify you after receiving the order, and you can then change the unit cost on the purchase order screen. The dollar amounts from the purchase order transaction are not recorded in any GL or inventory accounts until the goods are received. When ordered items are received, you can retrieve the purchase order (using the "enter receipts on purchase orders" selection from the "activities" menu) and mark which items have been received, adjusting the unit cost if necessary. At that time, the purchase is posted as an increase in inventory and an increase in accounts payable.

Figure 11-6: *Inventory purchase order*

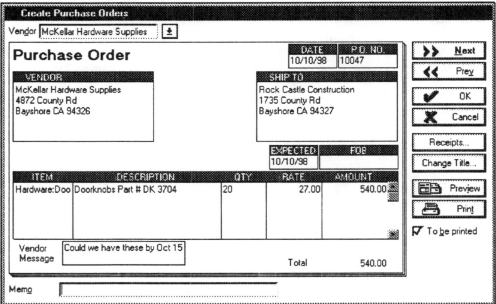

Alternatively, the purchases transaction entry screen, described in detail in Chapter 5, can be used to enter data from invoices that have been received for inventory items that you purchased without creating a purchase order (possibly by phone or purchasing for cash). The inventory reorder report (shown in Figure 11-13) should list, in a separate column, the number of units on order for inventory modules that track purchase orders so that you can follow up with a vendor if you do not receive the items in a timely manner.

Inventory Costing Methods

Computerized inventory systems usually recalculate the unit cost of each item in inventory every time a new purchase is made or an adjustment is entered. QuickBooks does this on the basis of the average cost of all the units on hand at the time of the sale. One-Write Plus has no capability for calculating and applying unit cost. Peachtree offers you the choice of three different inventory costing methods: average cost, LIFO (last in, first out) or FIFO (first in, first out). If you are using Peachtree and are not sure what method to choose, ask your accountant. The average cost method is perfectly acceptable for most businesses. Here is how it works:

You bought 8 kitchen sinks for $50 each on January 10 (total cost of $400). You buy 2 more sinks on February 28 when the price has gone up to $55 each (total cost of $110). For the sake of simplicity, let's assume that you have not sold any of these yet. The average cost per unit would be calculated as:

Average Cost   =   total cost divided by number of units in stock

January 10 - $50 = $400 / 8

February 28 - $51= $510 / 10

Please note that the average cost stays closer to the original $50 unit cost than to the newer $55 unit cost because we bought more units at the lower price. If one kitchen sink is sold on February 28, the average cost of $51 would be the amount deducted from inventory and charged to cost of goods sold.

Peachtree is the only package that uses LIFO and FIFO; see the user's manual for a detailed explanation.

Selling Inventory

Once the inventory is on the shelves and in your computer file, you will want accurate and quick preparation of sales invoices when you sell those goods. The preparation of a sales invoice was covered in Chapter 5, but let's focus now on the use of the inventory master file in this document. Figure 11-7 displays the sales invoice transaction screen from QuickBooks so you can see how the sale of an inventory item is billed to the customer.

Figure 11-7: *Sales invoice for inventory*

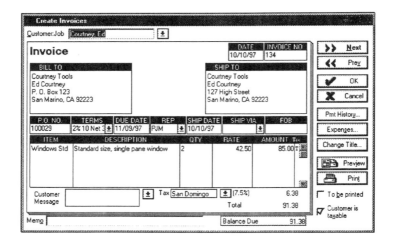

Sales Invoices for Inventory Sales

The date, invoice number, terms, and bill-to address are all filled in automatically once you type the first few characters of the customer name (in this case, Courtney). When you click in the "item" field at the lower left half of the invoice, a list of inventory items drops down; when you select "windows:std" from the item list, the description and unit price are automatically pulled into the invoice. Type in the "qty" (quantity sold) and the software does the rest, calculating the extended price and appropriate sales tax based on the tax code associated with that customer. (The software entered the $42.50 unit price, $85 line total, $6.38 sales tax, and $91.38 total in Figure 11-7.) You can, of course, add many items onto the invoice, including labor and service items, and include a memo and customer message. When you are satisfied with the look of the invoice, you simply click on "print" or "OK" to post (copy) the transaction to all appropriate accounts.

Posting of an Inventory Sale

When the invoice transaction is posted in GL accounts, the sales price is recorded in the sales revenue and the accounts receivable accounts, while the cost of the goods are recorded in the cost of goods sold and the inventory accounts. Figure 11-8, a transaction journal for just the one sales transaction from Figure 11-7, was produced by QuickBooks to illustrate all the parts of a transaction entry for the sale of merchandise. This is accomplished by displaying the sales invoice on the screen and selecting "other" from the "reports" menu; then selecting "transaction journal"—the transaction journal that is produced reflects only the one sales invoice that was on the screen. This QuickBooks report is an excellent way for novices to "see" the results when they are first starting out with accounting tasks. You would not normally print this single transaction journal on a regular basis.

Figure 11-8: *Sales transaction in journal form*

			Rock Castle Construction			
			Transaction Journal			
			October 10, 1997			
Date	**Num**	**Name**	**Item Description**	**Account**	**Debit**	**Credit**
10/10/97	134	Courtney, Ed		Accounts Receivable	91.38	
		Courtney, Ed	Standard size, single pane window	Materials		85.00
		Courtney, Ed	Standard size, single pane window	Inventory Asset		30.00
		Courtney, Ed	Standard size, single pane window	Cost of Goods Sold	30.00	
		State Board of Equ..	CA sales tax, San Domingo County	Sales Tax Payable		6.38

The point being made with Figure 11-8 is that the invoice total of $91.38 (including sales tax) is debited to accounts receivable, while the sales price of $85.00 is credited to materials revenue, and the sales taxes of $6.38 are credited to sales tax payable. These two credits total $91.38. The unit cost of $30 for that window is credited (deducted) from inventory and debited (added to) cost of goods sold. This type of entry is made every time a sale of inventory is recorded. If there are many items on the invoice, the sale entry will be quite long.

Bar Code Scanning Systems

None of the low-end accounting software supports the use of bar code scanning equipment as a method of data entry, although most high-end packages have a module for this. If your business sells inventory that can take advantage of the Universal Product Codes (UPC) already on items, and you want to be able to scan items to be input for accounting purposes, then you will have to look for special software to handle this. You might still use Peachtree, QuickBooks, or One-Write Plus for your general accounting needs and produce summary inventory results from a retail scanning/cash register system.

Inventory Adjustments

Once in a while, you might need to adjust the on-hand quantities of inventory items, and even less frequently, you might want to adjust the overall or unit cost of the items. The latter might occur if you are a ski shop and in the late spring decide that you are going to sell a certain brand of snowboards for less than their cost. To recognize this loss on your records, you would reduce the unit cost of those snowboards to the projected sale price and charge this loss to a "liquidation losses" account instead of charging the whole cost to cost of goods sold.

After taking a physical inventory, you may need to adjust the quantity of items due to theft, spoilage, fire, or miscounting on an earlier inventory. When you want to increase the number of units, you enter a positive quantity and can enter the cost associated with the increased quantity (most likely using the current average cost from your inventory master file). This will cause an increase in the total quantity on hand and in the total value of the inventory. If you need to enter a negative adjustment, you won't enter a unit cost because the computer will calculate a unit cost that applies to those decreases just as though the items had been sold.

Figure 11-9 shows the inventory adjustment screen from QuickBooks where you specify the expense account that will be used for the adjustment (the offset to this expense is the increase or decrease in the value of the inventory asset account) and then type in a new quantity next to the item you want to adjust.

If you click on the "value adjustment" box, you can type in your own new value dollar amount; if you leave "value adjustment" unchecked, you can let the computer figure the new total value based on the additional number of units and the current average cost. Peachtree and QuickBooks handle inventory adjustments in the manner just described, while One-Write Plus adjusts only the inventory quantity but does not adjust the asset or expense account.

Figure 11-9: *Inventory adjustment*

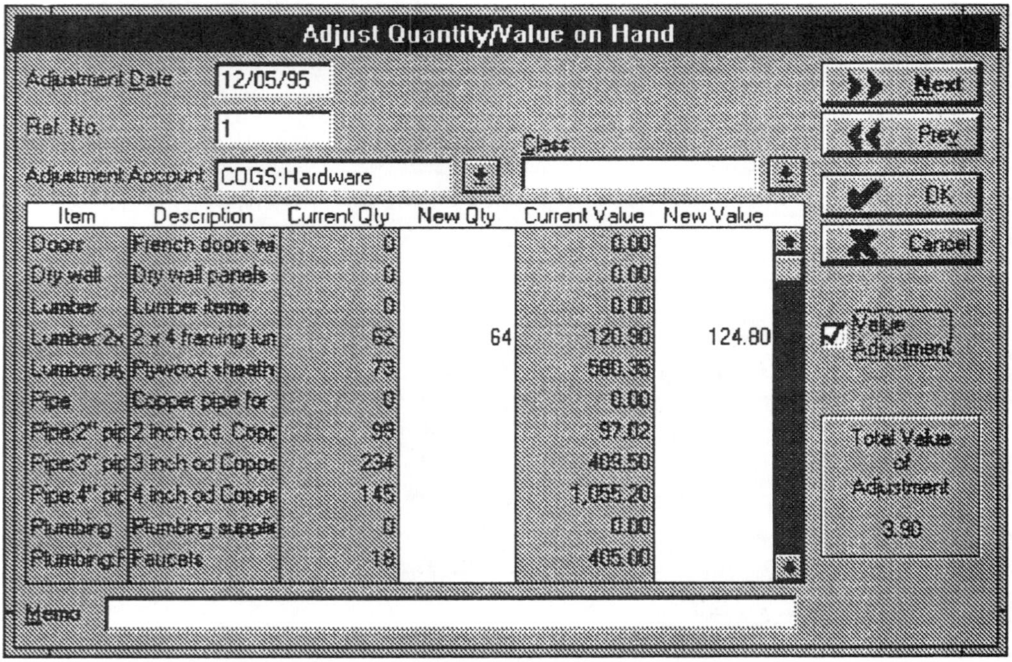

Inventory Inquiries

The most frequent use of an inventory system (other than to track the purchase and sale of items) usually entails your desire to "take a look at" the status of one, some, or all of the items that you have in stock. If a customer calls about the price and availability of an item, you surely want to be ready with a quick answer. Your accounting package with an inventory module should be able to instantly display the status of an item on screen in a manner similar to the QuickBooks Figure 11-10. This screen gives a quick view of unit cost, selling price, and availability ("qty on hand" and "qty on order"). Similar information can be seen on the Peachtree screen of Figure 11-3.

Figure 11-10: *On-screen inventory inquiry*

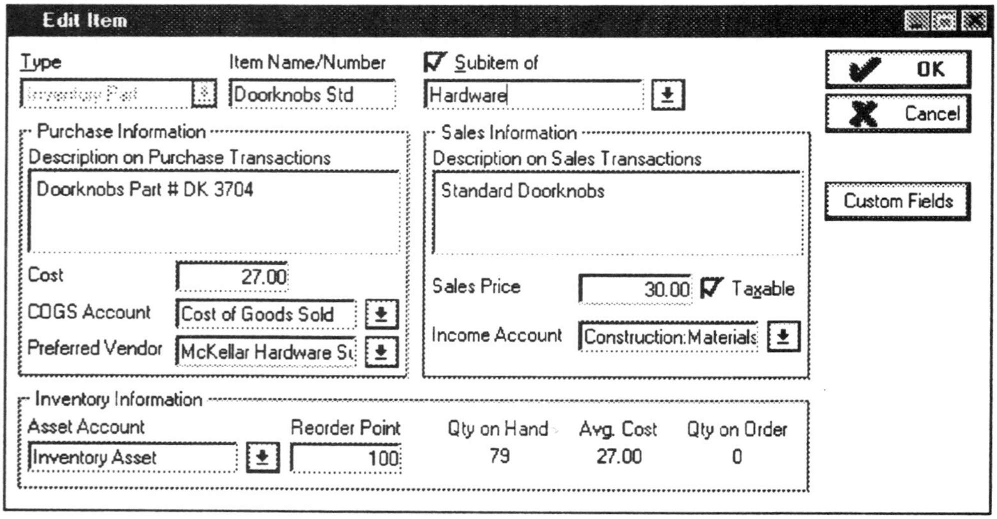

Inventory Reports

Reports that describe the status and activity of your inventory are the stock status report, the inventory ledger detail, a reorder report, and various inventory activity analysis reports. You will find many other inventory reports available in these popular accounting software packages. You should explore which ones will meet your accounting and management needs.

Stock Status Report

An abbreviated stock status report from Peachtree is shown in Figure 11-11 (not all inventory fields are shown). The main purpose of this report is to show the number of items in stock, the unit cost of the item, and the total value of that item as of a specific date. It is common to print this report at the end of each month. If you print the contents of the inventory ledger frequently (see below), you may find that you don't need the stock status report at the same date as the ledger report.

Figure 11-11: *Stock status report*

	Bellweather Cleaning Services Inventory Stock Status Report as of March 31, 1998					
Item ID	Item Description	Qty on Hand	Min Stock	Reorder Qty	Avg Cost	Item Value
A001	A1 Cleaning Fluid	6.00			3.00	18.00
A100	Ammonia	99.00			3.00	297.00
BT.5MIL-4QT	Plastic bags; .5 mil; small	16.00	25.00	30.00	6.72	107.50
BT1MIL-13	Trash bags; 1 mil.	19.00	25.00	30.00	5.20	98.80
BTW-20091	Cleaning clothes; box of 100	11.00	10.00	15.00	4.96	54.51
BWST-3QPL	Plastic Waste Basket	42.00	10.00	15.00	2.56	107.55
C1500-105FL	Floor Wax; Vinyl floors	32.00	25.00	30.00	3.75	120.00
C1500-150FW	Polish; Marble Floors 1 GAL	20.00	3.00	4.00	7.67	153.42
C1501-255QT	Glass Cleaner	39.00	15.00	20.00	2.50	97.50
C1505-FP9	Furniture Polish	32.00	15.00	20.00	4.04	129.25
C1600-208GN	General Purpose Cleaner	13.00	15.00	20.00	2.37	30.87
C1700-300HS	Hand soap; liquid	34.00	15.00	20.00	2.50	85.00
C4000-110FLC	Floor cleaner; General	64.00	10.00	12.00	7.44	476.00
C4000-200WD	Wood Floor Cleaner	53.00	15.00	20.00	8.90	471.70
C4000-230QT	Disinfectant Spray	86.00	15.00	20.00	1.10	94.60
KIT-1000	Cleaning kit; standard	4.00	5.00	6.00	11.19	44.74
KIT-2000	Cleaning kit; heavy duty	5.00	5.00	6.00	29.02	145.09
P1004-911M	Paper Towels; Carton of 12 pkg	53.00	25.00	30.00	7.70	408.00
P1005-98B	Paper Towels; Rolls	37.00	15.00	16.00	9.10	336.70
RBIN-100F	Recycling Bin; Plastic	53.00	25.00	30.00	7.47	395.80
RBOX-3P	Recycling Carton; 3 ft.	31.00	25.00	30.00	2.69	83.45
						3,755.48

Inventory Ledger

The inventory ledger is like a customer or vendor ledger—it keeps the history of all transactions affecting inventory and groups that data by inventory item. When you print the detail of the inventory ledger, the report will list the purchases, sales, and adjustments for each item and show the ending balance for the item. A sample of the inventory ledger detail report is shown in Figure 11-12. QuickBooks calls this the inventory valuation detail. Because we are concerned with both quantities and total value of the inventory, this report must show the quantities and dollar value after each date shown on the report.

Reorder Reports

A good inventory system should inform you when the quantity of an item falls below the acceptable level that you want to keep in stock—this was discussed earlier in this chapter under "purchase orders." The most common way to do this is

Figure 11-12: *Inventory ledger detail*

Type	Date	Name	Qty	Cost	On Hand	Avg Cost	Asset Value
Lumber	11/30/95						
2x4 Studs	11/30/95						
Bill	12/15/95	Horst Whole...	40	78.00	102	1.95	198.90
Invoice	12/15/95	Crawley, Do...	-10		92	1.95	179.40
Inventory Adjust	12/15/95		-2		90	1.95	175.50
Total 2x4 Studs	12/31/95				90		175.50
Total Lumber	12/31/95				90		175.50
Plumbing	11/30/95						
Faucet	11/30/95						
Invoice	12/15/95	Crawley, Do...	-1		17	22.50	382.50
Total Faucet	12/31/95				17		382.50
Sink	11/30/95						
Invoice	12/15/95	Crawley, Do...	-1		-3	21.00	-63.00
Bill	12/15/95	Tunic Plumb...	4	98.00	1	24.50	24.50
Inventory Adjust	12/15/95		0		1	20.00	20.00
Total Sink	12/31/95				1		20.00
Total Plumbing	12/31/95				18		402.50
Windows	11/30/95						
Std Windows	11/30/95						
Invoice	12/5/95	Courtney, Ed	-2		43	15.00	645.00
Total Std Windows	12/31/95				43		645.00
Total Windows	12/31/95				43		645.00
TOTAL	12/31/95				151		1,223.00

Rock Castle Construction
Inventory Valuation Detail
December 1995

to establish a periodic date for printing an inventory reorder report that points out items that meet the condition: quantity on hand is less than the minimum quantity needed. Unfortunately, Peachtree and One-Write Plus do not produce such a report—you can scan the stock status report to highlight those items with a quantity on hand that is too low or, in Peachtree, you can rely on the "action alerts" described earlier in this chapter. The reorder report provided by QuickBooks is shown in Figure 11-13.

Activity Analysis

There are usually a variety of inventory activity reports that you can try out to determine which best suits your needs. Sales activity causes inventory

Figure 11-13: *Inventory reorder report*

Rock Castle Construction
Inventory Reorder by Item
as of August 10, 1994

	Reorder Pt	On Hand	On Order	Next Deliv	Order	Sales/Week
Doors	0	0	0		X	0
Dry Wall	0	0	0		X	0
Lumber						
2x4 Studs	100	62	100	8/3/94		8.1
Plywood	45	73	0			11.7
Lumber-Other	-1	0	0			0
Total Lumber		135	100			19.8
Pipe						
2" pipe	100	99	40	8/20/94		21.9
3" pipe	100	234	0			3.6
4" pipe	150	145	60	8/18/94		12.9
Pipe-Other	-1	0	0			0
Total Pipe		478	100			38.4
Plumbing						
Faucet	10	18	15	8/20/94		1.6
Fittings	25	57	25	8/20/94		4.5
Sink	10	-2	8	8/18/94	X	0.9
Plumbing-Other	-1	0	0			0
Total Plumbing		73	48			7

(this is a partial report)

reductions and expenses of COGS—the cost of goods sold journal helps you track these sales. An inventory item activity report analyzes purchases and sales by comparing one period to another and calculating percentage increases and decreases. An item activity report can sometimes be grouped by customer, by salesperson, and/or by inventory category with subtotals and percentages to help you track what proportion of your sales comes from each group. An inventory profitability report shows the revenue from sales, the total cost of those goods that were sold, and the calculated gross profit for each item in inventory (and should report the calculated percent of gross profit on that item). I think this last report is the most helpful and revealing for an inventory-oriented business, so I have chosen the profitability report from Peachtree for your examination in Figure 11-14. You should explore the usefulness of the other reports described above.

Figure 11-14: *Inventory profitability report*

<table>
<tr><td colspan="6" align="center">Bellweather Cleaning Services
Inventory Profitability Report
For the Period From Mar 1, 1995 to Mar 31, 1995</td></tr>
<tr><th>Item ID</th><th>Item Description</th><th>Units Sold</th><th>Sales($)</th><th>Cost($)</th><th>Profit($)</th><th>Gross Profit(%)</th></tr>
<tr><td>BT.5MIL-4QT</td><td>Plastic bags; .5 mil; small</td><td>7.00</td><td>78.75</td><td>47.04</td><td>31.71</td><td>40.27</td></tr>
<tr><td>BT1MIL-13</td><td>Trash bags; 1 mil.</td><td>6.00</td><td>46.20</td><td>31.20</td><td>15.00</td><td>32.47</td></tr>
<tr><td>BTW-20091</td><td>Cleaning clothes; box of 100</td><td>21.00</td><td>157.95</td><td>104.05</td><td>53.90</td><td>34.12</td></tr>
<tr><td>BWST-3QPL</td><td>Plastic Waste Basket</td><td>16.00</td><td>70.62</td><td>40.97</td><td>29.65</td><td>41.99</td></tr>
<tr><td>C1500-105FL</td><td>Floor Wax; Vinyl floors</td><td>3.00</td><td>18.75</td><td>11.25</td><td>7.50</td><td>40.00</td></tr>
<tr><td>C1500-150FW</td><td>Polish; Marble Floors 1 GAL</td><td>12.00</td><td>145.20</td><td>92.05</td><td>53.15</td><td>36.60</td></tr>
<tr><td>C1501-255QT</td><td>Glass Cleaner</td><td></td><td></td><td></td><td></td><td></td></tr>
<tr><td>C1505-FP9</td><td>Furniture Polish</td><td>26.00</td><td>137.75</td><td>105.03</td><td>32.72</td><td>23.75</td></tr>
<tr><td>C1600-208GN</td><td>General Purpose Cleaner</td><td>11.00</td><td>34.10</td><td>26.13</td><td>7.97</td><td>23.37</td></tr>
<tr><td>C1700-300HS</td><td>Hand soap; liquid</td><td>42.00</td><td>135.54</td><td>105.00</td><td>30.54</td><td>22.53</td></tr>
</table>

(this is a partial report)

Item Listings

There are many types of item listings; they can be as simple as a price list with just the item name and the sale price or as complex as a full inventory master list containing all fields from the inventory master file. Since most software allows you to customize these reports, you can decide which fields you would like to see on your item listings.

Taking a Physical Inventory

Having the computer track and report on your inventory does not relieve you of actually going out on the floor (or to the back room) periodically to take a physical inventory. This means that you will take a hands-on count of each item. Most small businesses do this once a year during their slackest time. It is at this time when you discover spoilage, theft, and small errors in the amounts that have been added to and deducted from inventory by your computer. Both Peachtree and QuickBooks provide a report called the "physical inventory list" which lists all inventory, in any order you specify, with a blank line where you and your employees will enter the physical count. These lists usually include the sale price of each item to help you identify the appropriate item. It is best to leave the "quantity on hand" off these lists so this number does not influence the people who are doing the counting.

After the physical count is complete, the handwritten counts can be compared against an inventory stock status report for the same date to determine where adjustments are needed. You should adjust the computer records to match the actual physical count. These adjustments are entered as described in the "adjustments" section earlier in this chapter.

Backing Up Your Data

Have you made a backup copy of all your data lately? Certainly after you spend considerable time counting inventory and making adjustments, you won't want to lose that data. You know; you've heard it before; you should make backup copies of data files every day! So just one more reminder—use the backup procedure that is built into the software or develop your own—but do it! The procedure and an illustration of the screen from Peachtree for Windows during the backup process was illustrated in Chapter 2, "Choosing and Using Accounting Software." Please read that section again!

Appendix

Sources of Information

Association of Small Business Development Centers
(headquarters of the National SBDC's)
1300 Chain Bridge Rd., Suite 201
McLean, VA 22101
1-703-448-6124

BestWare, Inc.
(owners of M.Y.O.B. for Windows and Macintosh)
300 Roundhill Dr.
Rockaway, NJ 07866
1-800-322-6962
www.bestware.com

CompuServe On-line Service
(vendor forums for specific accounting packages:
One-Write Plus, MYOB, QuickBooks)
500 Arlington Center Blvd.
P.O. Box 20961
Columbus, OH 43220
1-800-487-9197
1-800-848-8990
or 1-800-848-8199 (for a sign-up kit)
www.compuserve.com

Computer Associates, Inc.
(AccPac Easy general ledger package)
One Computer Associates Plaza
Islandia, NY 11788
1-800-225-5224
www.cai.com

Computer Discount Warehouse
(mail order house for software)
1020 E. Lake Cook Rd.
Buffalo Grove, IL 60089
1-800-473-4239
www.cdw.com

CTS, Inc.
(accounting software evaluation guides)
11708 Ibsen Dr.
Rockville, MD 20852
1-301-468-4800
www.ctsguides.com

DacEasy, Inc.
(owners of DacEasy Accounting)
17950 Preston Rd., Suite 800
Dallas, TX 75252
1-800-322-3279
www.daceasy.com

Faulkner & Gray, Inc.
(publishers of Accounting Technology and Electronic Accountant)
11 Penn Plaza, 17th
New York, NY 10001
1-800-535-8403
www.faulknergray.com

Great Plains Software
(owners of Great Plains Profit)
1701 38th Street SW
Fargo, ND 58103
1-800-926-8962
www.GPS.com

Intuit, Inc
(owners of QuickBooks for Windows and Macintosh)
P. O. Box 3014
Menlo Park, CA 94026
1-800-446-8848
www.intuit.com

Medlin Accounting Shareware
(owners of PC-GL, PC-AR, PC-AP, etc.)
1461 Sproul Ave.
Napa, CA 94559
fax: 1-707-255-4475
www.community.net/~medlinSW/

M-USA Business Systems
(Pacioli 2000 accounting package)
2611 West Grove, Suite 106
Carrollton, TX 75006
1-800-933-6872

One-Write Plus/Peachtree Corporation
(owners of One-Write Plus)
20 Industrial Park Dr.
Nashua, NH 03062
1-800-649-1720

Peachtree Corporation
(owners of Peachtree Accounting for DOS, Windows, or Macintosh, and
One-Write Plus for DOS and Windows)
1505 Pavilion Place
Norcross, GA 30093
1-800-228-0068
www.peachtree.com

PC Connection
(mail order house for software)
528 Rt. 13 South
Milford, NH 03455
1-800-800-5555
www.pcconnection.com

PC Zone
(mail order house for software)
707 South Grady Way
Renton, WA 98055-3233
1-800-258-2088
www.pczone.com

Platinum Software Corporation
(owners of Access to Platinum software)
195 Technology Dr.
Irvine, CA 92618
1-800-999-1809
www.platsoft.com

Small Business Administration
(small business advocates and services)
1441 L Street NW
Washington, DC 20416
1-202-205-6600
www.sba.gov

Small Business Computing
(Small Business Computing magazine)
P. O. Box 59902
Boulder, CO 80322
1-800-537-4638

State of the Art Software, Inc.
(owners of Business Works Accounting)
8211 Sierra College Blvd., Suite 440
Roseville, CA 95661
1-800-447-5700
www.sota.com

Glossary

A

Accrual basis accounting

Method of recording revenue when it is earned and expenses when they are incurred, even though cash changes hands later.

Aged accounts

The technique of listing balances in accounts (usually customers) based on the age of the due date when money is owed.

Assets

Things of value that a business owns, like cash, equipment, and supplies.

Average cost

An inventory approach that calculates the cost of one unit by dividing the total cost of all units on hand by the number of units on hand.

B

Backup

The action of making copies of your data files to be stored away from the computer in case of a computer failure or other emergency.

Balance sheet

The financial report that lists what the business owns, what the business owes, and the value of the owner investment.

C

Chart of accounts

List of account names, numbers, and descriptions identified as necessary categories for financial statement reporting.

Closing

Removing the detailed data in accounts at fiscal year-end; especially important for employee payroll records.

Conversion	To convert your data files from one form of software to another.
Cost of goods sold	The original cost of the inventory that is being sold.
Credit memo	A document that results in a decrease in accounts receivable that provides the evidence that goods have been returned or an allowance (adjustment) is being made.
Credit	The right hand column of an account, where additions to liabilities, owner equity, and revenue are recorded; and where decreases in asset or expense accounts are recorded.

D

Debit memo	A document that represents a transaction requiring a decrease in accounts payable; this usually involves the return of goods to a vendor or an allowance (adjustment) against amounts owed to a vendor.
Debit	The left side of an account; an increase in an asset or expense account and a decrease in a liability, owner equity, or revenue account.
Defaults	Internal settings within computer software that are used to perform automatic procedures until you change those default settings to suit your own preferences (e.g., the margin settings in a word processor).
Double-click	Quickly clicking the left mouse button two times.
Drill-down	To look behind the lines on reports for details about the amount on that line.

F

Filters (on reports)	Applying selection criteria in order to restrict the information shown on a report.
Finance charges	The penalty charge you apply against a customer balance that has been left unpaid beyond the due date.

G

General Ledger (GL) The set of accounts that a business has identified as the financial items it wants to track.

Generally Accepted Accounting The accounting profession rules for recording
 Principles (GAAP) financial transactions.

Gross margin The difference between the cost of an item and its selling price (also called gross profit).

H

Hardware The physical, electronic parts that make up a computer system (e.g., the monitor, mouse, etc.).

I

Income statement A financial statement that lists all revenue accounts and all expense accounts, subtracting the expense from the revenue to determine net income or loss.

J

Journal An accounting document where the effect of transactions are expressed as debits and credits and listed in chronological order.

L

Liabilities Debts or amounts that a business owes to outsiders, like accounts payable and notes payable.

M

Module A subsystem of an accounting system (e.g., the accounts receivable function is a module).

N

Net profit The difference between revenue and expenses.
(also called net income)

Network	Two or more computers, linked electronically, that share data.

O

On-the-fly	A software feature allowing the user to enter a new customer, vendor, employee, inventory item, or account while in the midst of entering a transaction.
Operating system	Software that controls the working parts of your computer and interprets the computer software.
Owner equity	The combination of the owner's investment in a business, plus (or minus) the earned net profit (or loss).

P

Payables	Amounts of money owed on account to suppliers or vendors.
Periodic inventory system	Recording purchases of inventory in an expense account, and delaying the recording of the cost of goods sold until a physical inventory is taken periodically.
Perpetual inventory system	Tracking inventory by adding every single item purchased to the inventory account at the time of purchase and subtracting each item as it is sold.
Physical inventory	Actually counting the inventory that is on the shelves or in the store rooms and warehouse.
Point-and-click	1. Using the mouse to activate a choice like selecting the icon that represents a program or function (e.g., start QuickBooks, or print a report); 2. Using the mouse to check (use) or uncheck (ignore) choices.
Pop-up lists	A table of choices that appears on screen as though it had "popped" out of a box; this occurs when a field on screen can be filled by selecting an item from existing choices.

Posting	Data is copied from screen transaction into accounts in a general ledger; in the accounts, the amounts are added to or subtracted from previous balances to determine a new balance.

Q

Query	To request a specific subset of data from your accounting records (e.g., displaying the activity for a particular customer only).

R

Read-only	Information that may be retrieved but cannot be altered. Your accounting software is read-only, but the data you enter can be changed.
Receivables	Amounts of money owed on account by your customers.
Recurring transactions	Transactions that occur regularly requiring similar entries in your accounting records (e.g., paying the rent each month).

S

Software	The collection of detailed computer instructions (called a program) that leads the electronic circuits through the steps of processing raw data into useful information.
Software vendor	The company who holds the license to sell a software package (e.g., Intuit, Inc. sells QuickBooks).

T

Terms *(selling or purchase)*	A brief phrase that describes the time frame in which a payment on account is due (e.g., 2 % 10, Net 30).
Toolbar	The choices arranged in a line of icons across the screen that represent features or procedures. The toolbar may change as you move to different screens.

Trial balance	A list of the ending balances in each account in the general ledger.

U

Unit price	The selling price of one unit of product that is offered for sale.
Unit cost	The cost of one unit of product that is purchased from a vendor and held for resale.
User groups	An association of computer users with a common interest (e.g., accounting software user group).

V

Vendor	An individual or business from whom we purchase goods.
Vendor Ledger	A collection of accounts where each account records the transaction activity for a vendor.
Voucher check	A disbursement check with a tear off section used for indicating the reference numbers, discount amounts, and net amounts of the items being paid.

Index